Sasha Noodle
STRING THEORY

a

MEMOIR
and

OTHER
STORIES

To Anderson —
I Hope You
Enjoy My Story
Best Wishes —
W/AH

D0802101

FOREMARK PRODUCTIONS • CARMEL, CA

Sasha Noodle String Theory: A Memoir and Other Stories

by Wanda Straw

© 2021 Wanda Straw

Published by Foremark Productions

Cover Concept by Wanda Straw

Cover Design and Illustration by Agnieszka Kaźmierczak

Cover Production Assistance by Cheryl Winningham

Book Design by Chris Molé

Portrait Photography by Agnieszka Kaźmierczak

ISBN: 978-0-578-78593-6

First Edition

Printed in the United States of America

for Eric

CONTENTS

PART THREE - After Sasha

PART ONE

BEFORE SASHA

*The Earth is not the center of the universe...
and neither are we.*

<small>NICOLAUS COPERNICUS
AND *THE THEORY OF THE SUN*</small>

IN THE SHADOWS

WHEN I WAS THREE YEARS OLD, I was so afraid of my shadow I would actually walk along the side of buildings so my shadow would not appear. I remember pressing myself along various walls feeling terror, walking like I was on a tight rope of death, carefully placing my feet against buildings in order that I would not be exposed to the sunlight and the possibility of seeing "it." I don't remember the first time I saw my shadow, but I do remember that once I knew it existed, nothing else mattered. In my young mind, I truly believed my shadow wanted my life. I didn't think the two of us could coexist or be a singular reality. During this brief period, I spent most of my waking life trying to outmaneuver and outthink my dark nemesis. My shadow controlled my destiny. I was only somewhat free of it at night, but in the darkness, shadows only seemed to deepen and multiply, even though less visible.

After watching me, yet again, walking along the side of the barn leaning desperately with my back against the building, arms and legs stretched out in complete panic as though my life depended on it, my grandmother finally took control of the situation at their Pennsylvania farm. She had been observing my behavior and fear for several weeks and finally said reassuringly, "Your shadow is never going to bother you again, and you will never be afraid, but you have to do what I say."

I was locked in my best defense position. Arms, legs and hands spread out wide like the star at the top of a Christmas tree, wide-eyed with panic as I looked to where she was standing. My heart was racing, and I was literally holding my breath. There was her shadow standing right behind her. I couldn't believe she could let herself be so exposed. There was no escape for her. I was determined she was not going to see mine.

"Just come to me, Wandie, and we will kill your shadow. It will never bother you again."

I didn't believe her, but she said it so convincingly, and my mother was standing next to me whispering such support, that, after a while, I decided to venture out into the light to see my darkness.

"That's great!" my grandmother said as I stepped toward her.

"Ok, there is your shadow. Do you see it?"

I nodded my head and clung to her leg.

"You are going to kill your shadow by stepping on it. Go ahead, just step on it."

And I did, though fearfully. Tentatively, I gingerly stepped on my shadow. Surprisingly, there was no resistance or consequence. I couldn't believe it. After a few minutes, I was stomping with a vengeance. I stomped the life out of my shadow. The tiny, dark figure went down without much of a fight.

"See, you are bigger than your shadow, and you always will be. You did that all by yourself."

She was so proud of me, but not as proud as I was of myself. I had killed my nemesis and felt an enormous relief. I had killed my dark side, and that gesture was now the biggest victory in my young life. It was my first lesson in the power of self, as well as the power of light. It was also an early indicator that perhaps this little shadow killer was more than a bit sensitive.

THE WILD CARD

Sasha Noodle String Theory was born on 10/10/05. I have always sensed that numbers are important, but I didn't realize they could change your life until much later. Let me be very clear about the next point. I am not a cat person, or at least I wasn't and never, ever thought I would be. I always silently felt sympathy for people who adored felines. Their devotion was so extreme and strange to me. How could anyone love an animal so indifferent, strong-willed and independent? I always thought of myself as a dog person. It was where my animal resumé was most proficient.

When I was young, we had a three-legged Dalmatian named Duke, who put up with my two siblings riding him like a horse in those early years. I feel very bad about that now, but we were young and at times lacked sufficient empathy and common sense. In my own and my siblings' defense, he seemed to enjoy giving us rides, though he never gathered much speed during those ventures. My great-grandmother, who babysat us occasionally, always made him a huge pancake from the leftover batter from our breakfast. He loved those pancakes and most likely thought they were rewards for the hardships he endured, namely the three of us. Yet, we loved him with the innocent devotion only children can feel, and when he disappeared suddenly from our lives, we wept with tears only children have the domain rights to own.

The transition to appreciating cats was a non sequitur I never saw coming. I was going through a tumultuous and extremely difficult time in my life. In the span of two years, I lost more than I thought possible. It was a royal flush of loss with a seven-card draw, and even though I know that is not a legitimate hand, it was the hand played to me. I once read that the most stressful situations to deal with are the loss of loved ones, the loss of relationships, the loss of a home and a change in one's job. I had every card in that deck. I may not be a poker player, but I know when the cards are stacked.

In the course of two years, from 2004 to 2006, I had lost my best friend to complications from AIDS, my grandmother (one of the true loves of my life), my partner of fourteen years (again, one of the loves of my life), my father, my home of eighteen years, and the owners of the high profile restaurant I managed, who are very close friends, and who had their contract bought out by the even higher profile hotel that owned their lease. I also lost someone who had made a difference for a memorable moment, and then was gone with great consequence, and then eventually none. Seven losses, seven cards. Numbers matter.

I had been living in California since I was in my late twenties. Throughout my early life, living in California was never an option I considered a possibility or a desire. In fact, I was rather adamant and falsely opinionated about not wanting to live there. Still, California would come across my radar throughout various times in my life, and it seemed to loom mysteriously, like an unspoken yet conscious thought. It was almost as though I knew on some intuitive level it had already staked its claim on me.

Before living in California, the closest I came to interacting with the Golden State was in sixth grade when my classmates and I were paired individually with a United States city for a writing correspondence excercise regarding tourist information. The project was to teach us formal letter writing for business and possibly to retain some useful geography facts. I was paired with Oakland, which seemed disappointing in its lack of glamour in comparison to its companion city of San Francisco, but the government employee, who in my eleven-year-old mind most likely sat in a basement office forced to read and respond to thousands of schoolchildren's forced and feeble attempts at civic writing, proved to be a solid and consistent letter-writing pal. Even though I lacked enthusiasm in my initial correspondence, it was exciting to my sixth grade self to actually get mail from the city of Oakland. The first brochure had a picture of the Bay Bridge, and I was completely intrigued. Oakland and I wrote to each other often after that, and I kept the brochures they sent me for a long while, though we disconnected wordlessly in one of my many moves in my twenties when I began to separate childhood memorabilia from my young adulthood.

The first major move of my life was so emotionally traumatic that the lingering aftereffects caused change to be systematically difficult for the rest of my life. Change is difficult in general, but I seemed to have come into this world feeling life with an unusual level of trepidation and resignation. There is a black and white photo of me at the age of two sitting on Santa's lap in full winter two-year-old garb, including Yogi Bear mittens, wool coat and a tassel knit cap. I have the saddest look in my eyes, even though Santa is smiling stoically. The look in my eyes seems to say, "I can't believe I am here again."

The speculation to feel hurt, the premise of what will cause the pain, and the problematic outcome has always been too much for my imagination. My anxiety and apprehension with change came early in my life when my family moved to Indiana from my homespun childhood in Pennsylvania. There had been small changes in my life up until that point, but this was emotionally traumatic and dramatic to a level I had never before been exposed. It was an entirely new experience. It was change on a deep and personal level. The move left an imprint on my psyche that forever associated change with hurt and loss and extreme grief. Yet, it also taught me the strength and growth that change can bring.

When my family moved to the Midwest during my junior year in high school, I was given the choice by my parents to stay and finish the semester (and the basketball schedule I was a serious part of as a starting forward on a team that was undefeated), with their promise to come for me at Thanksgiving—or I could move with them in September on the official family moving day. The choice was mine, but I was paralyzed with guilt and other emotions. The movers were literally outside my bedroom, and I couldn't decide. I could hear them approaching every hour, but I could not make the decision because I didn't want to disappoint my family, but I also didn't want to disappoint myself. Every time the movers got closer, I cried with more intensity and angst.

When the boxes were outside my bedroom, my mom came in and sat on my bed and said softly, "Honey, they need to pack your room. What do you want to do?"

I was crying profusely and an emotional mess, but I listened for the first time in my life to my intuition and heart.

"I want to stay, but I don't want you to be upset with me."

"Then that is what you should do."

And that simple statement made all the difference in that moment and gave credibility for most of her other words for the rest of my life. From that moment on, I trusted her to understand the truth and to believe and trust in me, even when we would disagree. It was the first time I saw my mother through adult eyes and her looking at me as an adult as well. It changed our dynamic for the rest of our lives. Trust is a bond, and once it is established, landscapes and contours change, even though the parameters fluctuate. Life is a rhythm of trust and suspicion. And it is one of the foremost dances between mothers and daughters.

I decided to stay and, in my naivete, bank my bets that my parents would realize their bad decision and be hauling everything back to Pennsylvania by Thanksgiving. Obviously, forgoing my age and naivete, I was not a gifted poker player. When they came for me on the holiday two months later, I was devastated. They were not moving back, and I was giving up my life at sixteen to go to some-place that seemed foreign and without a soul, without a soul that had any connection to mine.

I cried the entire way across Interstate 70 through Ohio. Despite my sadness about leaving my relatives and friends, what also kept the tears flowing was the fact that I couldn't believe that many corn-fields could exist anywhere. The cornfields extended as far as the eye could see in every direction except for the straight edge ruler of the highway. It seemed like an alien landscape. I had grown up with mountains and rolling hills and highways that were as dangerous and exciting as an amusement ride. Nothing had prepared me for the monotony of I-70 through the Buckeye State. Every time I tried to stop crying, I looked out the window, saw the vast ocean of empty fields and started sobbing again. Indiana proved to be no different; corn was the eternal landscape, though I learned to appreciate it years later and value the soul that it resonated.

My West Coast bias was most likely grounded in my prideful, youthful East Coast suspicions that nothing of real significance trans-pired past the Pennsylvania/Ohio border. The rolling miles of flat cornfields only seemed to confirm that skepticism. As painful as change can be, it never disappoints in what is eventually found and discovered. The move to Indiana laid a foundation of distrust and fear in change, but it also made me understand that very good things can eventually come from taking a leap of faith and moving forward.

Destiny and the passage of time were always on my young mind. As a child I was unusually obsessed with time and how we pass through the space of our lives. On the eve of turning ten, I was throwing a ball against the side of our hundred-year-old brick walled house in Pennsylvania and catching the ricochet response in my baseball mitt. We rented the top floor of the house and the attic and half of the basement of the massive older haunted structure. I have a distinct memory of that moment of playing catch with the building and thinking to myself that everything was going to change now because I would be ten tomorrow. Double digits and it would be downhill and more responsibility from that moment on.

"Nothing but heaviness from now on and I will be a changed person. Everything will be different starting tomorrow," I remember thinking to myself. And even in that moment, as serious as it seemed to me, I knew intuitively this was not a normal thought for a ten-year-old.

It was also not normal at a young age to be concerned about hearing my heartbeat and pulse when my ear was on my pillow as I was trying to fall asleep. The sound of my blood pumping through my body, and hearing it through my ear when it was pressed firmly against my bed, made me suspicious and anxious, but eventually secure. I have always had an uneasy relationship with sleep and the loudness of my inescapable heartbeat seemed to mock my restlessness in the night. Most nights when I was young, and sometimes later, the sound of my heart beating through my body filled me with anxiety about the shortness of life and my imagined inability not to be able to do enough with the time and passage given to me. The sound of my heartbeat when I was trying to sleep was a constant source of worry and anticipation. How I balanced fear and expectation became a study in meditation and resolve, especially at a young age. Mostly, I stopped listening when I realized my heart was going to keep beating and pulsating in my ears as long as I continued to listen to it. When I learned to accept its vigilance, diligence and duty, I stopped fighting the fear. I eventually learned to accept and not listen except when I needed to know being alive was exceptional despite the circumstance. The beating of my heart in my ear against my pillow eventually became a whisper of hope and promise. And a whisper is the closest thing to the truth.

Still, the excitement of gaining passage, despite my concerns, was also hopeful and even thrilling, even with my worrisome nine-year-old self weighing the possibilities of becoming ten and stressing about the outcome. Having sadness over the passage of time, yet being intrigued with the outcome of new possibilities and the hope of a better and more meaningful existence, became a constant thread throughout my life. I have always had a love/hate relationship with change, but for some reason I take that anguish to the point of personal expectation and discourse. It was torturous how much pressure and expectation I put on myself throughout college and my young self and even much later. When I was very young, I would stress to the point of making myself ill if I didn't know exactly how to get somewhere when I hadn't been there before. Going to an alternate site for music lessons or other activities brought on a seizure of questions, until I knew in my mind I wouldn't be lost and had a sense of control over the situation. Having control has always been a priority. And it would be for much of my life, until I had none. We all have our lessons. It took a seven-card draw of immense loss and grief to make me finally understand how the loss of control can eventually liberate and free and eventually save. Sorrow is a masterful leveler.

From 2004 to 2006, absolutely everything I knew to be true and real about my life left without warning or notice. It was as though my life slowly and exactly imploded. One of the peripheral hurricanes of those many storm fronts in 2005 told me about a cat at her father's veterinary clinic that needed a home. She told me this cat was exceptional and that I needed to bring it to my new single person living home. I stalled and evaded and avoided making a decision. This was December of the worst year of my life, 2005 to be exact. I moved into my new-but-old Carmel cottage rental a month later in January, and in the midst of dealing with so much loss and so much newness, she called and said simply, "When are you bringing your cat home?"

I had visited him a few days prior at the vet's office. The staff seemed completely taken with "Tang," their name for him because he was an orange tabby. Every time one of them mentioned his name, I noticed they smiled as though they were in on a secret. I saw him from a distance at the front desk. He was in a cage a good distance from me, yet when he looked at me, he stood up on his hind legs and stretched. Around his lips he had what appeared to be chocolate lipstick. It wasn't chocolate though, it was just him and his amazingly weird, beautiful face. He seemed indifferent to everything but me and yet bored at the same time. His look is what lingers from that first encounter. It said simply, "I belong with you whether you want me or not."

When the tech, who happened to be the Hurricane's brother, brought him to me, he talked about Tang and how special he was and that he, also, was not a cat person but that this little orange guy had really gotten to him. I suspected a sales pitch, but he is the no-nonsense one in his family, and he sounded sincerely struck. I picked up the soon-to-be-named Sasha and held him. I did the kitten test for temperament, which I had learned from the aforementioned gale front, which entails holding them on their back suspended in the air to see what they do. He stretched for miles and hung upside down and just waited for me to make the next move. He looked into me for a few seconds and then seemed to cop an "it's your move" attitude. I didn't hesitate, even though I had no idea what I was doing. I was completely numb from so much loss and change I wasn't thinking or feeling very much at all lately, and when I was feeling, the circuit breaker was constantly overloaded. I was just trying to get by each day, and even though a choir of "no" was singing through my cavernous self, I heard myself say, "Yes, I'll take him home tomorrow."

"Not today?" the calmer version of Hurricane asked.

"No, I'll get him tomorrow."

I had just left my eggshell-lined comfort zone of many years, and any new change now needed some time to process. I needed a day to ease into it because that is what I do. It is what I always do. I move forward but prefer to hesitate for a second right before takeoff. I may move through life in an older car but with a heavy foot on the accelerator. Still, I had just done something completely against my better judgment. I went home to withdraw and prepare and not think about anything forthcoming; the present was already too much to carry. Yet, I knew I needed something completely new to counter the tremendous loss I was feeling. I just wasn't ready for it to begin today.

The reason I was hesitant to adopt Sasha was because I had already agreed to take/keep/adopt (terms were modified later) Sal, the Hurricane's beloved black two-year-old feline. He was the first cat I ever truly connected with and found interesting, though I was sympathetic to Buffy and Miss Kitty, two cats that Seth, my youngest brother, nurtured and loved throughout the last years of our parents' tenure. I was coping with learning to be a pet guardian, but at least I had the luxury of taking that class with a smart, not-a-kitten-anymore cat. Sal was incredibly special in his intelligence and free will. He was easy to love and trust. He made me think all cats are independently loving and true and easy to adopt. Words of advice to the novice pet owner wannabe: Do not fall for the following words from even those you trust and share ice cream with, "Having two cats is as easy as having one. They practically take care of each other."

Yes, and Iraq in the summer is a nice place to take a vacation.

THE SASHA JOURNAL
TO HELP KEEP ME SANE

M Y CLOSEST FRIEND, AGNIESZKA, has suggested I keep a journal to try to put my frustrations and supposedly humorous insights somewhere. When I told her I was just a little frustrated, she smiled slightly and showed up a few days later with a Moleskine journal. She always has the best intentions and the most ardent results.

February 16th

Sasha came home three weeks ago. The first thing he did was kitten hop to Sal with a huge smile on his face. I swear it was a smile, and it was illuminated with his chocolate lips. I never knew what a kitten hop was until that moment. When kittens run they hop out of sheer joy or enthusiasm or some other thing we can't name or know. All I know is you feel their exuberance just by watching them. Sasha seemed so incredibly happy to be anywhere but where he was before, in purgatory, waiting to start his life. I remember thinking that it isn't every day you get to bring a kitten home, and for a wonderful short while, that was all that mattered.

Sal has taken to the big brother role extremely well. The Hurricane told me, with a bit of sadness in her voice, it would change his raucous, independent personality, and it seems it has a bit. They are both on the raw food diet, and feeding time is like throwing bait to sharks. They eat in fifteen seconds or less with Sasha usually honing in on Sal's bowl before he has even finished his own, thereby making certain he is privy to at least part of Sal's food and his own, which is still waiting for him. Sal never takes Sasha's food, ever. If it seems he has been shorted because of the orange rover, I always give Sal more and keep Sasha away either by holding him or taking him to the office and shutting the door. Feeding time is the closest I will probably ever come to small or big game hunting.

Except for the feeding madness and the feeling of constantly being in the middle of a World Wrestling Cup competition, life is new and interesting and even charming. I am letting Sal out a little bit each day to scope his surroundings. Taking care of the two of them is definitely helping to keep the focus off of how bad I often feel.

March 1st

Sasha loves strings. Let me rephrase, Sasha has a string fetish. He is absolutely crazy for them. Agnieszka was wearing ballerina shoes with long laces and Sasha was so enamored with them he seemed like a schoolboy in love. She couldn't keep them on her feet while she visited because he never stopped trying to undo them. Ever since the string fetish manifested, he lunges at anything that resembles strings of any kind. He tackles ribbons just because they happen to be in the same family as a string. He does not care. He does not differentiate. He just loves the loose ends of life. I don't understand how he could be my cat. Loose ends define my life right now, and I take no sense of pleasure from them.

I bought a pair of boots that require a good deal of lacing up and I can't put them on in front of him because he attacks and worships and becomes obsessed. I will be walking across the room to sit in a chair to lace the strings, and, suddenly, he has them in his mouth causing his entire body to be dragged along as I walk, which he seems to thoroughly enjoy. I look at him in his young life and his long legs and short body and chocolate lips smile, and he seems so sure of who he is. Sometimes, I swear, he looks at me like he is just waiting for me to understand who he is and who he is not. Maybe I am being too sensitive here, or maybe not enough. He looks at me so intensely, sometimes, I feel like I should know him or something about him I am not getting. He is a kitten, yet he feels like one of the oldest souls I have ever known.

March 11th

I suppose I should explain his name…Sasha because I wanted something with an S to go with Sal. Sasha because it seemed gender neutral. Sasha because it was military and mysterious and gay sounding all at the same time. Sasha because, when I said it, I felt him. Noodle because my nine-year-old friend, Daisy (my close friends, Tony and Tricia's daughter from Sierra Mar, the owners of the restaurant I manage) was given the responsibility of giving him a middle name. She has a formidable reputation for a no-nonsense but humorous turn of phrase pet naming. She has named all of her family's pets. Notably, Biggy and Littlely, their two Siamese longhairs. They are both very fat and similar looking to each other, and in all my time spent at their house, I've never heard a guest correctly match name to animal.

When I asked her, "Why Noodle?" she said simply, "Because," and added a few seconds later, "I like it."

That was all it took for me. Daisy's pet naming talents were legendary, and I considered her to be a bit of a visionary. I can relate to that and trusted her completely.

"Noodle it is, then."

String Theory was added later because it just had to be so.

March 22nd

Pulled up to the house today and heard furniture crashing, and for a second thought maybe someone had broken in and was trashing the place. As soon as I started walking down the stone walkway to the house, everything got very quiet. When I opened the door, it looked like a tornado had blown through, and not one feline could be found. One of my favorite vases was shattered near the fireplace. It had been knocked off from the mantle and pieces of jagged glass lay spread over the entire living room. As I was cleaning up and verbalizing how appalled I was at their behavior, Sal and Sasha quietly and sheepishly emerged.

"Seriously, you two, it sounded like there was a heavyweight wrestling match going on in the house when I drove up. How can you possibly make that much noise? And how did this vase break?" I swear when I looked at Sasha, his chocolate lips were smiling.

April 3rd

Sasha keeps sleeping on the gas stove. I scold him when I catch him doing it, but I know he is doing it when I'm at work because I find orange hairs on the stove. My mom is worried he is going to turn the gas knob by accident and burn the house down. He must like how warm the top of the stove feels. He doesn't yet sleep on the bed with Sal, and sometimes I see him looking up at us, and he has a sad look in his eyes. In fact, his eyes are usually either excessively filled with emotion or completely devoid of any. I'm starting to think he is either mentally impaired or incredibly brilliant. I honestly don't know in which camp to put up stakes.

April 9th

Carmel residents love their dogs and cats. It took me a while when I first moved here to get used to the lengths of devotion they have for their animal companions. Cats in baby strollers, small dogs in bicycle baskets, large dogs with scarves around their heads in the front seat of convertibles are not uncommon sightings. Carmel was founded in the early nineteen hundreds as an artist community, and evidently, the locals' affection and affinity to animals stretches back to the origin of the town and through its entire history. Stories about the bohemian artist's beloved dogs and cats are well documented in books and photographs. Mary Austin, Jack London and Sinclair Lewis represent an esteemed but very short list of the many artists, some successful but most struggling, who contributed and shaped the colorful and unique history of the town. Even today, Carmel has an artistic temperament and a rebellious side. For most of the town, there is no mail delivery to homes, which explains why the post office, for those residents, poses as a social outing or political gathering at times. There are no chain restaurants and no streetlights or sidewalks except for the main part of town, and the streetlights are actually antique looking lamps, which cast a soft insight instead of a harsh reveal. There is even an old law on the books that prohibits women from wearing shoes with heels higher than two inches.

Carmel has always maintained an independent spirit. Perhaps it was in that vein that Doris Day bought the Cypress Inn in the late eighties and turned it into a haven for animal lovers and their pets, usually canines. During high tea service on Saturday afternoons, from noon till three, Terry's Lounge often has more canine guests than human. Dogs of every breed, size, weight and personality fill the lounge during the formal tea service. It is not unusual to observe a St. Bernard sitting calmly next to a Chihuahua as their guardians sip tea, nibble on tea sandwiches and petit fours while exchanging the latest local fodder.

Carmel Beach is one of the most beautiful beaches in California. It is a long white sand expanse that stretches dramatically until it ends at the Pebble Beach golf course. On any given day, there is a bounty of every type of dog imaginable enjoying the beach along with their guardians. On Sundays there are dog groups based on breed, which get together to have play dates and bonding time. The first time I saw this I was taken aback by how many groups there were and how excited both guardian and dog seemed to be by just spending time with each other. It seems the dogs are catching up on their week while their adult counterparts do the same. It made me realize they have a support group and I could definitely benefit from one for felines. It would be so good to have some sort of measurement for Sasha's behavior, but then maybe I don't want to know his percentile ranking of normalcy versus extremely eccentric behavior. A Sunday support group for felines would probably confirm the growing suspicion that Sasha stands alone in his uniqueness. In that respect, Carmel is perfect for him. And for me as well.

April 12th

Sal and Sasha's wrestling matches are shaking the house and my nerves. My house is a vintage bohemian-style Carmel cottage with hardwood floors, a fireplace, the original gas stove and heater and over a hundred medium-sized pane glass windows. From the moment I first saw the house, there seemed to be a familiarity and understanding between us. The cottage is surrounded by three old California oak trees and a huge pine tree in the front yard near the street. Carmel is only one square mile in diameter and originally was known for its quaint, small, rustic cottages on rather modest lots. Yet, the lots in my neighborhood are large for my nine hundred square foot abode, so there is a substantial amount of yard in the front and back of the house and a fair amount surrounding the sides. (Many of the houses surrounding me have been rebuilt and claim their entire lot size.) My rented cottage was built in 1945 and made out of California redwood lumber in a single-wall construction style, so when Sal and Sasha decide to playfully rumble, the entire house rattles from the effects.

I have developed a new timeout technique when the wrestling

matches get too extreme. I put one of them in the office and the other one in the living room and shut the glass door that connects the two rooms. So, when they get a timeout, they can see each other. Sasha gets so distressed looking at Sal through the glass that I don't make the timeouts very long. Today when I came back to the room to end their penalty time and open the door, Sasha had figured out a way to get his paw under the door, and they were holding hands. I felt like the enemy I was and vowed to only use timeouts when I thought they, the house, or I was in mortal danger. I need a bigger combat zone.

April 20th

Sasha has not yet learned how not to use his claws for everything he wants. Since he is a "jumping hugger" specifically aiming for either my thighs or my neck, and since both areas contain large veins vital for the movement of blood to and from the heart, I have been bloodied a bit lately. Making a note to myself to ask the vet if this is a stage or another Sasha abnormality. Also making a note to get more peroxide and Band-Aids.

April 26th

Woke up this morning and several pieces of my jewelry and all of Sasha's strings were laid out perfectly straight by his water bowl. Everything had been washed and some of the items were still wet. They were laid out like they were on display to be purchased at a flea market. I looked at him for a long time and he just looked back and held my gaze. "Who are you?" I whispered to myself and quietly started to have a vague feeling of knowing.

April 29th

Sasha is finding his voice and it is getting stronger every week. Sal is a musical virtuoso, and his voice resonates beautifully when he purrs. He practically sings when he is happy. Sasha has always been on the quiet side until recently. Now he sounds like a choirboy with his voice about to change from puberty. The other day I swear he said, "Hello." He was drawing it out so that it started like a meow, but it changed so many notes it had remnants of an aria. It ended on a high note, which sounded a bit like exasperation. I will get a second opinion but I know "hello" when I hear it. It was eerie and fascinating at the same time. After I got over the strangeness of it, I had to smile. I don't really know much about cats, but this one is off the charts strange. I have felt like he has been trying to say or convey something to me since he came to the cottage. My cat said "hello." Am I losing my bare string of sanity?

May 9th

When I woke this morning, Sasha was sitting by the bed looking at me. He had a strange look of sorrow mixed with defiance. I am realizing I am giving too much attention to Sal, probably because I knew him first and have never known cats before, hence the safer connection. I am starting to realize I need to focus more on the orange Tasmanian devil in my life and let him in closer. I am struggling so much to get through the day-to-day with everything else I am feeling. Most days it takes all of my energy just to keep up the pretense that I am fine. Work is demanding and I have a position with huge responsibilities as well as managing over forty employees. The feeling of loss and change weighs on me like an anchor. Am I not paying enough attention to him? Is that why he is becoming more verbal? Once again, I find myself wondering who he is and what he is trying to say to me. My own words are restricted and in need of an outlet, but even if I had one, I don't think I could utter the words that matter. Maybe "hello," but maybe not yet.

Mother's Day

Decided to walk to the beach and took my cell phone with me to call Mom somewhere on the journey to let her in on this glorious day. It was quintessential Carmel on a clear, warm day and it was spectacular. Carmel is nestled within a forest of pine and oak. The homes and streets meander and yield to thousands of trees, and the effect is magical. When the sun shines, there is nothing but beautiful, distinctive homes and trees, endless flowers of every color and variety, breathtaking shoreline and the bluest sky. It is ridiculously quaint in the best way possible. I call my mom while coming back from the beach and tried to share the moment. She is talking and I am listening, the familiar pattern, the way of time. The way it has always been. As I walk to the door, I notice a huge dead wood rat with a missing head just beyond the porch. Sal is close by, nonplused and proud, staring into conqueror warrior tribunal space. I freak out, but my mother is a saint on this day of mother worship. She has been and continues to be a master of mother-speak. She talks me through the clean up, the why the head is missing discussion and the reasons why this could be a good thing. She is laughing gently at my timidity. She is a mother and a friend and never judges my skittishness, at least outright. She grew up on a farm and has not a skittish bone in her body. Her laughter, mingled eventually with my own, is what lingers.

The diposing of the "body," which I forced/begged on Agnieszka, is also what stands out. The true sign of friendship is knowing you can count on body disposal and they never judge, and she never did and never does. When Sal was missing during his three-day disappearance, and my backyard was a jungle of weeds and plants, Agnieszka came over because I saw a black object in my yard. The overgrowth was so high I couldn't tell what it was, and because I am a squeamish yardstick of fragility, I asked her to uncover the black object. It was actually an enormous dead bird; Sal was still a possibility of hope. As she held up the large black raven and smiled, I knew she was my friend for life. I have a severely difficult time with dead objects, and my Polish lifeline does not. The image of her knee-deep in weeds and flora, while holding that dead bird and rejoicing it was not Sal, will always be an unusual but cherished postcard in my life.

May 27th

Woke up early in the morning to go to the bathroom and had a strange sensation something was wrong. I was groggy so it took a few minutes to realize all of the throw rugs from the bathroom were gone. When I went to the kitchen, I realized two of the rugs from that room were also missing. Around Sasha's water bowl was literally a fort made of rugs. It was a perfect circle of protection. It was a perfect statement of ability and craziness. He had arranged them so they were half standing on their own. Inside the fort was his water bowl but also a quaint and, I felt, very personal selection of his favorite strings and toys. All of the items had been washed, of course, and were drying nicely in the early morning light. It must have taken him all night to drag the rugs there and arrange them in such an orderly and comfortable fashion.

I've given up trying to understand his increasingly interesting and bizarre escapades, but the surprise element is definitely in his favor. I stood in my cottage kitchen, in my new life, surrounded by my cozy but still strange to me little wooden house, and my old life, the one I had grown into and out of for fifteen years, fell away a little more. In the quiet dawn of morning, an orange kitten was taking up fort building under my roof. For the first time in a very long time I started a new day with a quiet smile and a whisper of a laugh.

June 10th

I am feeling outnumbered lately. Tonight I was on the phone for a long time. It was a rare warm Carmel spring evening. Warm enough to have the windows open and warm enough to have a glass of wine outside while having a long phone conversation. Sal is going out every day, but I only let Sasha out under Sal's supervision. They are not allowed out after dark. When I took the phone outside, I knew they were in the house. Sal went in at sunset. The longer the conversation ensued, the more wine I drank. Suddenly, I noticed Sal running around the corner of the house with little orange guy in hot pursuit. Sasha had that chocolate grin lit up so well I could see it in the moonlight. I put the phone down and asked, "What are you two doing out here?"

When I opened the door, they ran into the house happily. I checked the house and closed the one remaining window, but it had a screen on it, so I thought maybe they snuck out when I had gone in for more wine. In a few minutes Sal came tearing around the house with Sasha doing the bouncy, happy run right on his tail. Okay, this is getting weird. In they go again. In I go again to see if I left the back door open. Out I go to finish my wine. Here they come again. I can see now it is a game, and they are having a great time. I finish the phone call and get serious about finding the escape route because if I don't I am going to be extremely freaked out. When I find the bedroom window open, I realize I was feeling the wine more than I thought. How did I miss that? They had never gone out the bedroom window before. I am realizing these two are made for each other.

June 22nd

So many of these journal entries could begin with, "When I woke up." Even though I haven't used that ominous statement often, this one requires that setting. It seems chaos loves the darkness. I woke up in the middle of the night because something seemed wrong. Something seemed uncomfortably different in the house. I sat up in bed, but the noise that woke me up wasn't there anymore. I never turned the light on because I didn't want to wake up completely. I have trouble sleeping and once I get there, I try to maintain the delicate balance between unconsciousness and reality. I called for Sal and Sasha and heard a faint stirring and some movement but decided I must have been dreaming and lay back down to return to wherever I had been. I went back to sleep quickly then woke up again a few minutes later. I thought I heard the sound of paper rustling. I sat up again and listened, but the house was quiet, eerily quiet, and I just threw it off as part of my overly active imagination. When I was falling back to sleep, I thought I heard paper rustling again and the cats in the bedroom. I let it go and just fell away.

Once again I will begin with ... When I woke up the next day, the first thing I saw was an empty wrapper of their raw food next to my bed. Let me explain the packaging and the gluttony. The raw food comes in a one-pound package cut into nine servings. It should last them two days at least. They, the perpetrators, are supposed to get one square inch twice a day. Because the food is raw, it is kept in the freezer since I buy so many at a time. I take it out of the freezer the night before it is needed and put it on the counter next to the sink to thaw out. I put it in a stainless steel container so the juices, if there are any, don't run on the counter. When I woke and saw the devoured, tattered, empty package next to my bed, I couldn't believe the debauchery. I couldn't believe the sneakiness and conniving trickery. I couldn't believe they could gnaw through a pound of frozen meat. I was utterly disgusted by the unsanitary grossness, but then lately I am living closer and closer to the obsessive-compulsive zip code.

When I came out of the bedroom with the stiff, well-licked wrapper in my hands and looked for the only suspects possible, what I found was two cats laid out pathetically on the couch next to each other barely able to move. They looked at me with an equal measure of pain and pleasure in their eyes. I held the empty wrapper in my hands. The empty wrapper which should have yielded two and a half days of food and simply said, "You are pigs."

Sasha's chocolate lips seemed to curve ever so slightly, but Sal looked worried and regretful.

"This is seriously disgusting and so wrong."

I realized at that moment I was talking to cats. Cats. "I am not a cat person," the voice inside my head was saying. Yet, the other voice was saying, "Damn it. Did you two really eat a pound of frozen food in the middle of the night?"

The latter voice was who I was listening to. The latter voice had all of the momentum.

"That is gross and so disgusting. I am not feeding you for two days."

I truly believed at that moment they looked at each other and a flicker of suppressed laughter was clearly visible. It was as though they were saying, "Dude, it was so worth it. And we really don't care."

If they could have high fived at the moment, I'm sure they would have. I am completely outnumbered and so utterly alone.

July 5th

Sal is missing. He went out in the afternoon and never came back. He will sometimes take off for an extended sojourn, but always comes home relatively soon after I call for him. Sasha is beside himself, crying at the windows and looking at me to make it right. I have called Sal's name for two and a half days and am increasingly distressed about his absence. I am incredibly stressed-out actually. His absence consumes almost every moment. I have been calling and walking and listening and am losing hope. I took tonight off at work because if he doesn't come home tonight, I don't think he can. As the night bears down, an intense feeling of guilt comes with it. Sasha spends most of his time staring out the front windows with an occasional glance at me of confusion, sadness and fear.

Around ten o'clock I am outside with my usual desperate calling and swear for an instant I hear something. I call again and hear a faint soft familiar voice, and it seems to be getting closer. A small shot of adrenaline fills my body, and I call again and now I know for sure he is close to the yard. Suddenly, out of the darkness comes a black small figure, and he is talking in notes of sheer happiness. Sal jumps up to me and I hold him as long as he will let me. He is looking through the door for Sasha and wriggles down to get to him in the house. Sal is home, and that is all that matters. The relief is immense. The two of them have a reunion, which will forever make me think and feel differently about animals. Sasha nuzzles his head under Sal's neck, and they quietly stay in that embrace for a very long moment.

They have souls. They have feelings. They love. And it is changing me.

July 6th

Sal has a puncture wound on his eye from his days away. The morning after his return, I took him to the Hurricane's father's veterinary clinic to get it diagnosed and treated. The Hurricane's father, Dr. Tom, is a holistic vet, and his skills are first-rate and remarkable. He treats Sal's wound and gives him fluids and gives me medicine to administer. This is new territory for me, but it goes well. Sal is so mature and so incredibly smart. I just talk him through it, put it in his food and it is painless for both of us. His eye waters often and may forever. I feel really bad about that, but Dr. Tom explains that Sal's eye is numb and the feeling could come back. Time will tell. It always does.

August 1st

After Sal's absence and return, after his wound and healing, something has shifted in the house and between Sasha and him. They still wrestle and cuddle and sleep next to each other, but there is a different feel to their interaction. Sasha was thrilled when Sal came limping back, but something has changed. Sasha has matured yet is acting out more than ever. I am doing research, and it seems he is positioning himself to be the alpha cat. He looks at me as though he is thinking about ways to get my attention, show me his acumen or simply make me mad. Sometimes he stares with a vibe so intense it crunches his eyes and face, and if he could talk, I swear he would say, "I am your cat. When are you going to get it?"

Still, the love between the two of them is genuine, and even though I am a stranger in their world, in all aspects of everything, it has never been this good, calm and promising so much.

I feel different as well. Healing happens in such subtle movements and shifts. For so long it is about carrying the sadness and just trying to find some small space or psychic niche where it is just slightly more bearable. Then one day you realize something is different. It is not a drastic change, yet it resonates in places within you that could almost be overlooked. But you recognize it because you have been holding on so desperately for a sign, some sort of sign of hope that will reassure you that this is not going to kill you. Maybe it happens when you stop looking and thinking about what you lost and don't have anymore and start trying, ever so slightly, to live your life now. When you look away from the beast and quit giving it so much power, the pressure of it bearing down on you feels just a little less and air comes into your lungs a bit easier. And you realize, for the first time in a long while, you are breathing on your own, and it has never tasted or smelled so good. Gradually, the hope and promise of other possibilities becomes a slow realization and a growing, gnawing quiet affirmation begins to sustain you and excite you and ever so slowly help you feel your life again. And the new life, even though it seemed like an eternity in coming, is finally overshadowing all that has been lost and what has been.

November 3rd

The Hurricane called. It is November and Carmel is blooming in autumn light and soft tones. A strange truce between Sasha, Sal and me has settled over the cottage. I don't feel so outnumbered. I don't feel outside the two of them or my life anymore. We have achieved a remarkable working relationship and existence. I returned the Hurricane's phone call even though I had a bad feeling about the forthcoming contents. The Hurricane wants Sal back. The Hurricane is going to play house with someone and wants Sal as an indoor pet in a studio in Oakland.

Sal is outdoor amazing. Sal is high in a gnarled massive tree staring at his domain amazing. Sal is big brother amazing. I remember a few months ago looking for Sal to bring him inside and seeing him high on the fading stark tree next door. He was lying majestically on a large branch. He looked like a black panther overseeing his territory. He is such a remarkable feline, and now he was going to be fodder for playing house. It doesn't seem fair to him. It is incredibly unfair to Sasha. It is heartbreaking to me.

Sal was the first cat I ever really liked and then grew to love. He was the first cat I ever felt a connection with and a sense of mutual respect and appreciation. This first year in the cottage, this very difficult year, Sal seemed always to have an eye on me in his nonchalant, yet knowing, way. I got very sick with the flu in March. It was the first time I had been sick and alone to deal with it in a very long time. I remember getting up from the couch to go to the bathroom, and I started to feel like I was going to pass out. Sal had also gotten up, as he was lying next to me, and was walking with me and staying close to my leg. As I started to get lightheaded, I felt him lean on my leg and then push into my leg with the top of his head. It was a considerable amount of pressure, and as I regained my senses a bit, I realized he was guiding me into the bathroom while making sure I didn't fall. He sat next to me while I used the bathroom, yet was gentlemanly enough to stare vaguely in the distance until I was finished. The return trip to the couch was the same. He walked slowly next to me, putting a bit of pressure on my leg with his body. After I settled onto the couch, I looked at him with tears of appreciation, loneliness and self-pity. He seemed to understand completely and stayed with me on the couch the rest of the day.

After much thought and consulting with close friends and family, I decide to let Sal go. I don't facilitate the move. On the specified day, it happens deftly all the same. I leave a key. The Hurricane comes in force. When I come home from work, he is gone. Completely. It is just Sash and I now, and the silence is deafening. The Hurricane always leaves a wake of silence and always will.

November 11th

I am trying to keep the mood light and optimistic, but for a week Sasha has been crying for Sal. He goes to the windows and cries. He looks at me while at the window and cries. His mournful tones echo my own feelings, but around him, I try to give comfort in long talks with short descriptions and no answers. It mirrors my own reality. When he sleeps, his eyes are furrowed like he is trying to solve a problem or is looking for something he can't find. I watch him in his restlessness and feel my own even more. I am not restless about the same things Sasha is feeling, but I understand longing for something that no longer exists.

November 15th

Sal has been gone for a week and a half. Sasha has stopped crying at the window and door. He stopped after a week, but the last few days he has been even more lethargic and sad. He has not been eating with his normal gusto and speed, but at least he is eating. I am missing Sal so much, but am worried more about Sasha and his frustration and temperament. He has been acting out and seems angry. He is scratching furniture, which was never an issue before. He is incredibly verbal but it seems sad and aimless. I am beginning to believe he is talking for both of us.

December 2nd

Stripped the sheets this morning. Sasha wanted to go outside, but I felt reluctant to let him out without Sal. This is new territory. I'm not sure I can trust him not to leave the yard, and I don't quite know how to be with Sasha without Sal. I am still trying to learn this new dynamic. He has been so verbal but also somehow calculating and mysterious in his moods and behavior. I took off the sheets and was getting the new sheets out of the chest. I went to the kitchen to get a drink of water and had a sudden feeling I should not have left Sash alone in the bedroom. When I went back to the bed, Sasha had peed on the mattress cover. Before Sal left, Sasha had knocked over another vase, which was special to me and full of flowers. I came home to glass shards everywhere, a dead flower smell and a defiant "what are you going to do about it" attitude. Before Sal left, Sasha would do almost anything to get my attention and was on a mission to seek and destroy. He has been intent for quite a while to be the alpha male. I am slow to understand what is sometimes rather apparent.

When I came back to the bedroom and saw the urine stain, I lost it. All of my anger about Sal being taken on a whim, all of my frustration with Sasha's acting out met a Celsius conversion point of propelled energy and anger. He was standing by the bed looking rebellious but also a bit unsure of his recent statement and deposit. His eyes seemed to be filled with anger, longing and sadness, but all I saw was the "fuck you" look in his demeanor. Maybe it was me and where I was, maybe it was his attitude, but I was done. I was over all of it. I went to the extreme place I seldom venture. I went to the place I don't believe in. I went to extreme anger and rage. His actions were such a deliberate violation, and he knew it.

He started to bolt, but I caught him on the neck and spewed my frustrations. I said, "No," over and over.

I said, "This is so bad and so wrong."

I said things I can't remember. I had him by the neck as he was scurrying out of the bedroom and threw him down the hall. In my defense, it wasn't a hard throw. I just tossed him onto the hallway, but it was intense and a life moment for both of us.

"I am done with all of it," I screamed and then sat down on the floor and cried for all of it.

I cried because I had lost my temper on an innocent animal. I cried because my bed had just been stained, and I was not even a part of it. I cried because I felt so alone and lost. I cried because I was overwhelmed by death. Eric Paul, my closest friend and confidant. My grandmother who was my love and anchor and my whispered prayer. The break up with my partner of fifteen years, which I thought would be forever. The change in ownership at work, who I consider two of my closest friends. Gone. Moving to a new space. A new home. The loss of love. The loss of her. Starting over and learning to be alone. Learning to listen to the silence and not be afraid of it. All of this in a span of two years, and at the moment of Sasha's bed wetting, it just seemed to come crashing down. It was the lowest point and a long time coming, but it finally happened and needed to be.

In my other life, I would never have known urine could be so life transforming. In my other life, I would never have thought any of this possible. As I sat in the hallway and cried, I knew the only person who could make this right was me.

SYMMETRY

HE DIED ON THE FOURTH. A perfect symmetry on the date of 04/04/04. He would have liked that, maybe on some level he even knew. He always orchestrated everything to the finest detail. Even when he was seemingly out of control, he seemed to have a plan for his madness, his crazy, insane way of looking at and living life, which only he understood. He always knew what he wanted even when he wasn't sure, even when he was completely immersed in the absurdity of his own creations.

I had never watched anyone die before this month, this day, this year. There is no mystic awakening or release. There is no poetry. He died fighting for his last breath. He looked terrified, eyes rolling madly, until he found Jose, his partner, and then he relaxed and listened to the one he loved, who was telling him to let go, that everything was going to be okay. He had been on a ventilator for three days existing somewhere between life and death, semi-consciousness and complete obscurity. He was in between reality, but I believe he was present on a level where no one could connect with him, but he could perceive what he needed. It is what I choose to remember because I could not reach him in his last days, but I could feel every part of him and who he was to me. I felt guilt for a long while because of my inability to understand what was needed and what was true.

Eric Paul never said the words AIDS to me until everything was beyond pretending anymore. I never asked him directly. I loved him too much by then, and with love comes profound respect and the understanding of silence. We spoke around it. We used other words. We spoke quietly of symptoms and new medications. He talked about the thrush in his throat, the herpes everywhere, the loss of sleep and the inability to eat. We talked about his lungs and the fungus growing rapidly in his right lobe. He was terrified of becoming a skeleton, an AIDS ghost clinging to a life that no longer existed except for the simple need to survive. Even in his frustration and fear and anguish, he never complained or asked for pity. He loathed that line of defense. He found humor on the surface of so much of it. He left me a voice message several months before the end. It was full of sadness and wry humor. It was Eric Paul personified.

"You know it is sad somehow that the only thing that makes me laugh anymore is the ridiculously high cost of my medications. There is something wrong in that, don't you think?"

It cost a thousand dollars a shot for a med he needed three times a week.

The voice message went on from there. It was softly intimate, and it was the first time I ever heard him really scared. I was driving from an appointment in Salinas and was so overcome by his voice, a whisper now on certain days, that I ended up lost, driving to Soledad until I found my way home hours later. He managed, somehow, to find humor in his body being overtaken by the throes of so many viruses his physical entity could no longer fight. I realize now, so much time later, his heart and spirit breaking was the ultimate demise and the beginning of the end. The end was so very different from the beginning. Throughout my life, I have found that what begins well usually changes to difficulty, and what begins as a struggle often evolves toward goodness. With Eric, both scenarios were true.

I met Eric Paul in 1996 when I went to work at Sierra Mar Restaurant at the Post Ranch Inn in Big Sur. Even though the world-class resort is perched high over the Pacific Ocean with stunning views and an A-list clientele, I was a reluctant recruit. I had been working at a restaurant in Carmel for a few years in a rebound work situation after leaving an upper management position with a company that did communication/audio-visual/media contracts with the government, which is the reason I came to the Monterey Peninsula. I was sent to Monterey to manage the company's contract at the Defense Language Institute, running a project that involved studio translation recording and audiotape production for every language on the planet in which the military and government had interests. Since this was the late eighties, the Russian school was the most prominent. How quickly that changed a few years later. The contract at DLI also included photography and graphic arts as well as satellite educational instruction, which was a new concept then. It was my fourth project as manager, though I was only in my late twenties. As for my newest government contract responsibility, the DLI project was extremely interesting. The institute overlooks the beautiful Monterey Bay and I was now living in the liberal "free to be you and me" state of California. The timing and temperament could not have been better for the change my life needed.

Initially, when the head of the company told me they were going to put in a bid for the Defense Language Institute and that would be my next assignment, I told him quite simply I had no interest in taking the position because I didn't want to live in California. He looked at me strangely then laughed a rebuke and said, "Why the hell not? Have you ever been there? It's where you should be living. You'll never want to leave if you move there." His voice trailed off softly on the last sentence.

A few months later when we were scheduled to do the walk through of the facility in order to place a bid, he did a remarkable but underhanded marketing campaign by flying me into San Francisco and bringing me down Highway One in a convertible. I remember being humbled, speechless and mesmerized. By the time I saw the dairy cows grazing next to the Pacific Ocean north of Santa Cruz,

I was utterly and completely smitten. I became obsessed with our company getting the DLI contract and after two years, we did. I had been moving every year for five years all over the country to start new project sites, and I had a feeling the Monterey Peninsula was a place I could maybe stay for a while. Then, after eighteen successful work and California fun-filled months, the head of the company wanted to relocate me to the East coast for another media contract. He had been right after all: I never wanted to leave the Golden State. And I didn't.

Because I didn't want to move back east to manage the start up of another government media contract, I was given an ultimatum. I had never walked away from anything before that decision. It was completely outside my comfort zone not to do what was expected of me, but I had been moving almost every year throughout my twenties because of college and work, and I was running on fumes. My brother had been killed in a car accident a few years before, and I had begun to realize I was using work as a means to bury my grief and avoid feeling the tremendous loss of him, even though those feelings consumed me. Work was the tangible reality holding me together. I was made Vice President of Operations when I was twenty-five. Even though the company was small, at the height of my tenure with them we had over two-hundred employees at four different project sites in different parts of the country. Work was the core of me. It always would be until many years later when I chose otherwise.

When I decided to stay in California, the company I worked for acted swiftly and decisively. Although we were "negotiating" the terms of my departure, they repossessed the BMW 325 company car which I had been given as a part of my salary compensation while I was in the shower one day. That car was my first real taste of adult success and I loved the feeling of driving it. It made me feel like I had something to show for the sacrifices of the work and my gains into adulthood. And I had. Yet, when I went, naively, to drive the car to the market after the shower, it was gone. Vanished, but a note was left in its place.

It said simply, "I told you so. You can't win here."

I was young and trusting and had no written agreements with them. I had lost the car and was not able to obtain unemployment compensation. I met with a lawyer in Carmel, a few blocks from where I eventually ended up working in a restaurant, and even though the verbal agreements I had with them should have been favorable to me in terms of compensation, without documentation I was left with nothing. The female lawyer was incredibly sympathetic and kind, but there seemed to be no recourse, and I felt crushed and outplayed in a man's game. I had no car, money or job prospects. I was living far away from my family and most of my closest friends.

The loss of my position and status, combined with the mounting grief over my brother's death, fueled a period of depression and anxiety. My mother came to see me during this time and gave me the best maternal advice of my life:

"You know, honey, no parent ever wants to see their child hurting. What happened to you was unfair and you deserved better, but you can't let this bring you down. You can't give up. You just have to use it to start something fresh and new. Until you figure out what you want to do, why don't you go work in a restaurant for awhile like you did in college?"

I remember looking at her and listening to her words and feeling her concern and love, and suddenly a huge weight seemed lifted. My life wasn't over. I had options. And those options would change my life.

Those options and circumstances are what led me to walk into the stunning restaurant at the Post Ranch on a beautiful April afternoon in 1996. Someone I worked with at the restaurant in Carmel and a close friend, Craig (who would eventually become the executive chef of Sierra Mar) was working at Sierra Mar and had called me several times enthusiastically telling me I should consider working there. I thanked him politely but told him I was hoping to get back into film and communications work even if it meant leaving the area, though the thought of leaving the Monterey Peninsula seemed dreadful and I could never consider it for very long. When I finally acquiesced to an interview with Tony and Tricia Perault, the owners of Sierra Mar, and their manager at the time, Eric, the view that greeted me as I entered the restaurant took my breath away. It was a quintessential spring day in April, so the spectacular, dramatic drive down Highway One was even more remarkable because of the striking colors of the abundant wild flowers that bloomed in the far-stretching ridges along the coast. Orange poppies, the state flower, and field lupines spread like a blanket above the deep blue of the Pacific Ocean.

When I finally walked into Sierra Mar, I was struck by the restaurant's sleek interior and impressive lines and décor. The restaurant had been built by Mickey Muennig, an architect of near legendary status in Big Sur and responsible for creating a style that was organic in approach and environmentally sustainable before the concept became a catch phrase. Sierra Mar is completely enclosed in glass from slate floor to wood beamed ceiling, creating the sensation of no barrier between the space inside the restaurant and the majestic view outside and beyond. At twelve hundred feet above the ocean, the power of the interaction is visceral and creates a physical reaction and sensation. I witnessed it many times with guests throughout my Sierra Mar career. People would walk into the restaurant and literally be overwhelmed by the sheer beauty of the panoramic vista. They would either be silenced in their awe or shout loudly in disbelief. It would become such a common occurrence that staff would often say to each other as they witnessed the various homage and reverence, "First time guest, I'm thinking. They've obviously never been here before." And then we would smile slightly to each other because one more person was in on the secret of the property and Big Sur.

Yet on that particular day in April of '96, I was a first time worshiper. As I walked to one of the walls of clear glass on the southern part of the building, I looked out at the Pacific Ocean and could see down the California coast for seventy miles or so and thought, "I could do this for a year or two."

It ended up being nineteen years and four months exactly. Numbers matter even when I didn't know their influence.

I vaguely remember my first meeting and impression of Eric Paul. I was standing at the host stand in the restaurant, and he introduced himself and welcomed me to Sierra Mar, yet he had the strangest look on his face. He was smiling at me, but his eyes were summing me up the entire time he was looking at me. It was as though his eyes and his lips were conveying opposite messages. He murmured something that sounded like "hello" and then walked away. After he left, someone next to me said, "Eric Paul runs the art program."

"What do you mean?" I asked.

"He selects all the art for the restaurant walls and picks the artists to have shows here. He is also a server, mostly at night."

"So he waits tables and also runs the art program? That's great."

"Yes, he is special," the person replied.

I wasn't sure how to take that comment. It seemed to imply many levels of affection and disdain at the same time.

My next memory of Eric is standing next to him in front of the service line at the pass window of the kitchen. The restaurant had an open kitchen, which meant you could see into the kitchen from the dining room. The engineering design of the restaurant was a constant source of admiration and functional/dysfunctional regrets. Due to the mechanics of the air system, the people in the kitchen could not hear a word from the dining room even if the servers were leaning through the pass window with their neck and head extended to ask a question or verify an order, but the guests in the dining room could hear every word and, seemingly, whisper from the kitchen. Since the dining room was a high-end dining experience and often romantically quiet, the noise from the kitchen could be disruptive and often embarrassing. In the early years of Sierra Mar, even though it was a unique, professional and intimate dining experience, the discipline of the staff on both sides of the house could be loose and a bit unorthodox compared to the usual rigid structure and standards of fine dining restaurants.

Case in point would be the story, which was whispered in hushed tones at the time of my hiring, of an employee being found butt naked at the infinity pool in the Big Sur morning light by a prominent, high profile guest. The restaurant employee was passed out and snoring from a night of after shift drinking. Eric Paul was already well known, for better or worse, for legendary misdemeanors. Yet, his ability not to get fired for his naked slumber only added to the wild west culture and his own enigma.

Eric Paul was a significant contributor to the mischievous yet harmful cohesion of discontent between the two sides of the house (dining room and kitchen). He seemed to thrive on creating a controlled environment of functional sustained chaos while promoting support and portraying innocence. Most of his antics were minor practical jokes targeted at select individuals. The surfers come mainly to mind. Yet, over time their annoyance with his continual "messing" with them evolved into a war of paybacks. It climaxed with the surfer faction, led by Marcus, replacing an amuse bouche of fava bean puree on toast points with an undiluted puree of wasabi on a toast point. They knew he was a habitual abuser of eating the amuse bouche starter. The preparation count of them was usually pre-determined based on the cover count of reservations for the night. We habitually fell short of those bite-sized bits because of the waitstaff eating those "mouth amusers," but the main culprit was Eric Paul. The wasabi replacement was a group endeavor. When he bit into the crostini, thinking it was fava bean puree with truffle oil and then realizing it was something specifically designed to set his mouth on fire, a small shift of power transpired. Despite the fact that his face grew red and actually swelled while still not giving in to the discomfort and pain to acknowledge defeat, his reign as the mastermind of chaos ended slightly and silently.

Yet another early memory of him in front of the pass window is distinct and specific. I remember it clearly because he made me uncomfortable. We were standing at the window waiting for food to come up, and he kept staring at me through his round black glasses with his hands clasped behind his back and a slight smile on his face. He had an affinity for finding people's personal or sensitive nerve endings and then poking that spot relentlessly when he felt the need or the inclination. Something about his stare was making me uncomfortable.

"Why are you looking at me like that?" I asked.

For several long moments, he did not answer the question.

"I'm just looking at you," he finally replied, smiling even more but in a goofy, strange way.

"Well, stop staring at me. It's starting to creep me out."

This, of course, made him more intent on staring more intensely. After ignoring him and then reprimanding him more, I turned my back to him. At that moment he came and stood in front of me, arms behind his back still and leaned into me and said softly, "I see you."

I was thrown off by his directness.

"What do you mean, you see me?" I asked quietly and nervously.

"I see you," he said again while smiling slightly and not breaking eye contact.

He said it so seriously and softly and with such sensitivity, I was completely taken aback. This was not the usual persona he presented to his world. This was a different mask completely. This was not the thorn in everyone's side when they least needed his combativeness. This was not the person who thrived on orchestrating chaos. Even though I was taken aback by his tenderness, part of me was not surprised. Even though I had been somewhat distant and suspicious of him in the beginning, I had become completely intrigued with how unusual and different his orbit seemed to be and how original he was in his approach to everything in his life. Eric Paul had an orbit around the sun that was discordant with the universe. He was a mystery. A brazen poem filled with sonnets and irreverent scripture and explicit vulgarity. He was Pan in his seeming refusal to grow up. He was Wendy in leather drag. He seemed to be an original voice and I found myself studying him while also being drawn to his unusual but interesting ways. Yet, his tenderness, when he said those words to me, seemed so close to the surface, he seemed to be giving a glimpse past the veneer. I realized at that moment there was something beyond the bravado and mischief, and it made me look at him differently. His words that day began a dialogue that became a connection of sorts then, eventually, something much more than a connection, and eventually a life changing experience.

After a few months of working at Sierra Mar, we began carpooling to work since we both worked the dinner service and had to be there at the same time for our shifts. More precisely, I was asked to join the small but prominent "all boys club" of commuters from town. This elite group included a few surfers (though mainly Marcus), who were actually waiters extraordinaire, a sommelier who could have been doing stand up comedy, Patrick, Eric Paul and me. Occasionally, there would be a stray fellow "townie" who needed a lift, but they were not part of the core group. I was the only female in the boys club, but they seemed to welcome a woman's presence into their testosterone-driven drives and conversations.

Carpooling with strangers five days a week for two hours per day is a quick remedy for not being strangers. There is something about being in a car, especially at night, and we were often driving home at midnight or later, that invites intimacy and trust and transcends the formalities of life outside the carpool. There are the carpooling roles, which exist within the car, and then there are the roles outside of the car. Yet, somehow the two realities coexisted while still being a separate reality. Even though I was reluctant to become a manager, I took a management position after a few months. It seemed a better path to a more consistent schedule while being able to assist in necessary changes in operations, and I was interested and curious about the operations. I was also falling in love with food and wine as a lifestyle and was eager to learn more. Still, my management role, though a silent shadow in the carpool, was not my carpool identity. We had a simple rule. What happens in carpool, stays in carpool. And it was always respected.

Eric was always intrigued with the El Sur Ranch at the Molera flats, which is the panoramic, majestic "opening" to Big Sur proper. One rainy winter night while driving home late from work, we realized the cows at El Sur Ranch had broken through a fence and were standing on Highway One in vast numbers and in various degrees of repose. Some of them looked elated with freedom but confused by the downpour. Others simply looked scared and confused. Upon seeing them, Eric Paul became nearly hysterical.

"We have to get these cows off the road!" he kept yelling in what was becoming near panic in his voice. "No one can see them! This is a bad situation," he kept saying over and over, which was making Marcus and me more nervous and determined, despite the downpour.

Eric Paul decided we were going to herd the cattle off of the road.

I would drive, and he and Marcus, a very capable problem-solver and dominant car pool presence, would herd the cattle to safety. The specifics of where to herd the many head of cattle was unclear since there was no safe place available in the torrential downpour and zero visibility. And so it began. He was getting soaked while he yelled at them in high-pitched, stress-driven broken Spanish and lurid English. I was driving slowly behind Marcus and him, frantically maneuvering my headlights to point where they are most needed. I try to tell him the word most effective for herding cows, but he is beside himself. He is not listening. My grandfather was a dairyman, and I remember, still, the magic catchphrases for getting a cow to go where needed. It is "soooowwwweeee," but Eric Paul is yelling noises that sound like rodeo calls by the clowns on horseback who retrieve injured cowboys from angry steers.

He is yelling, "Zooooot Zoooot! Hellibe Hellibe!"

Marcus is screaming at him through the wind and rain, "What the hell are you saying? You are scaring them more! What the hell is 'Zoot Zoot?'"

Eventually, after an eternal while, we realize none of the cattle will be saved by our stoic though feeble efforts. The cows are standing in the road in the downpour with their heads hanging low, seeming to succumb to their fate if destiny chooses. Marcus and Eric Paul come back to the car absolutely soaked and freezing in their wetness.

"That was just utter bullshit and a waste of time," Marcus says while trying to get warm.

"We made a difference, I think. At least they are all together on the road," Eric Paul counters.

"Yes, so now they can all be killed together," Marcus muttered while drying himself off with a towel from my swim bag.

We finally drive to the ranch house responsible for all those heads of bovine. Eric Paul is knocking loudly and repeatedly on their door. Water is falling off of him as he pounds impatiently. There is no answer for a long time and then eventually, I suppose what one may call a modern-day cowboy comes to the door in Ugg boots and cappuccino in hand. Saturday Night Live is clearly visible on a large format television in the background. Eric explains the situation but the Ugg boot cowboy is nonplussed and says simply he will "deal with it."

We drive away in the storm, but Eric is talking in sputtered acceleration, like only he can or could. "What are they doing watching Saturday Night Live? Did you see the cappuccino? He had Ugg boots on for Christ's sake. They don't care. Those cows are going to get creamed. It is raining so hard no one will see them. Where are real cowboys when you need them?"

And of course, that started a whole new train of thought and at least he was off the cows for a few minutes and focusing on the demise of cowboys in society and their fall from grace. Marcus and I breathed a quiet sigh of relief. They were soaked to the skin, but Eric was oblivious to anything except the cause, and we had failed in his eyes. Maybe we always did, because his expectations and measurements were so high but his actual reality was so mysterious and without definition, I never knew where his measurement for satisfaction really existed, until I knew completely.

For someone who appreciated cars as much as he did, Eric was absolutely consumed by the need to destroy any vehicle he drove. He never serviced his car, checked the oil, put oil or water in or worried about tires. He measured his love for his automobile by how much abuse it could take and not die on him. It was a common theme throughout his life. Black smoke often billowed from his cars, but he pretended not to notice. Eventually, I, and those few others who suffered, quit asking. Still, he would come excitedly alive when barking out the name of passing cars with relish and authority.

"Did you see that?" he would scream in the middle of some obscure soliloquy.

"No, what was it?" I would ask for the hundredth time feigning interest.

"It was a '67 Porsche streamlined, classic."

When other people were carpooling with us who were experts on cars, guys who took this stuff even more seriously than he did, they would call him out.

"You're smoking crack. That was not a '67. That wasn't even a Porsche. You're high. And what the hell does 'streamlined' mean?"

The banter would carry on endlessly, and I would pretend to read or disappear until a safer, more interesting round of exchange would eventually draw me out of my comfort zone. When the endless debate would pursue longer than I could bear, I would finally find my voice out of desperation and sanity requirements.

"Hi, remember me. I'm in the car, have been for the last half hour, and I don't know anything about what you are arguing about."

Genuine apologies would abound from every corner of our moving time capsule.

I used to think he actually was an expert on cars until I witnessed his demise by those who knew more. Again, it was another common theme throughout his life.

Somewhere in the course of getting to know Eric Paul, in the first few years of being more involved with each other's life, he offered to pick up my mom from the San Jose airport because I was scheduled to work and couldn't get my shift covered. It started so innocently. After listening to my dilemma, he said simply, "I can pick your mom up at the airport."

"Really? But is that putting you out? You don't know her, and I don't want to inconvenience you on your day off."

"I don't mind. It could be fun."

He said that statement with support but also with an edge of mystery and suspicion. Eric Paul could be a lot to absorb at one time, especially if you are not prepped. My mother could also be a big presence if you are not prepared for it. I thought about the two of them together and realized they would either become fast friends or their time together would be completely south of compatibility. I didn't have another option so I agreed to have him pick her up at the airport.

This was the late nineties before cell phones and the tracking of everyone's movements every moment, when real time was real time, and people actually had to coordinate events and timelines. I got home from work around 11:30 p.m. expecting to see my mom in my Monterey townhouse eagerly greeting me, but she wasn't there and there was no message on the answering machine. I had a beer and waited for them on the balcony. When 12:30 came and went, I was past being worried. Her flight got in at 7:00, so where were they now? I knew Eric Paul had an agenda with errands in San Jose, but this was late hours for my mom, and I was anxious.

I was sitting outside on my deck trying not to worry when Eric Paul's older Volvo station wagon pulled up to my carport close to 1:00 a.m. He emerged from the car smiling at me with that "got you" look. My mom came out of the car seeming a bit tipsy and looked up at me on the balcony and yelled, "Eric Paul kidnapped me!" and then started laughing that great laugh of hers.

"I told him you would be worried. Hi, honey! He took me for dinner, and then he got lost in San Jose. We had Mexican food!"

My mom doesn't really like Mexican food, but obviously he had wooed her with spice and charm.

"I wasn't lost, woman," he countered with a smile.

It was love at first sight for them. And remained that way.

On the way home, they played a favorite word game of Mom's at that time, which revolved around celebrities' names. The premise is to take the first letter of a famous person's last name that your competitor says and then use that letter for the first name of another celebrity you recall, but you can't use a name twice from any player. For example, Meryl Streep could be countered with Sam Shepard and so on. My mom is quite good at this game, and Eric Paul must have realized early on he didn't have a chance. Evidently, he resorted to porn star names and then, eventually, made-up porn star names. It took my mom a while to realize what he was doing because he can tell a lie with such a straight face and so convincingly it is difficult to challenge him.

After Eric unloaded Mom's luggage and was saying goodbye to both of us, the banter between them was still lively and affectionate. We were standing outside my townhouse well after one o'clock in the morning and they were still arguing about the game's outcome.

"Eric Paul, thank you for picking me up tonight and for dinner, and I'm sorry you got lost," Mom said laughing.

"I'm sorry I beat you at the word game, and I wasn't lost, lady."

"Eric, you cheated with those names. I never heard of any of them, and I go to the movies."

"Well, you must not go to all of the movies."

"Wanda, have you ever heard of an actress named Cherry Driver? Or Sac Ballentine?"

When I looked at Eric Paul and shook my head, but tried not to laugh, my mom pounced.

"Eric Paul, I knew you were making those names up! Or are they porn names? Oh my God, you were using porn names! Oh my God, you cheated with porn names. Porn names are a sin."

But she was laughing in spasms and crossing her legs, which I knew meant that she was trying not to pee in the wee hours of the morning.

Before he got in the car, he gave me a look and a special smile then said to my mom, "I would never cheat. Maybe you need to see more movies. Goodnight, Mama Shirl."

As the sound of his sputtering Volvo pulled away, and he headed for Carmel, Mom turned to me and said, "He is crazy, but I had a great night. I'm sorry if you were worried."

"It's ok, Mom. I'm glad you had a good time."

"Well, I just wanted to get home to you, but that Eric Paul, he had an agenda. He is something else."

Which is Pennsylvania speak for special, crazy, unique, wonderful and more.

One of Eric's biggest agendas and obsessions was art, and he had an incredible eye for it. Art was his passion, and it consumed most of his waking hours. It was believed by those who knew him best that his art business would either make him wealthy or put him in jail for fraudulent practices. I never, in all of my experiences, saw anyone more capable or criminal in sales. I know so much of it was method-acting, but he was so passionate it shaded all of the grey tones that left one wondering. He loved art, and he viewed his life through that one single lens.

I carpooled with him for nearly eight years, and many hours of our coastal journeys were filled with him pontificating about the smallness of the Carmel art scene, his frustration in dealing with artists and his love of them, the nuances of various art movements, both current and historical, and who he was courting or whoring into bringing art to some newly affluent dot-commer who had recently acquired a home on the Peninsula. He always insisted his love of art was foremost, but he loved money and finer things, and he had a honed sense for being attracted to and attracting himself to people who had both. He loved the hunt, and he thrived on the kill.

He could also confidently and with snobbery speak on the best watches to own, the demise of fashion, the latest in fashion and the most hip in cycling gear. (He took it up briefly, but longer than his kayaking phase and had the best gear both sports could offer.) Seeing him in activewear always left one wondering about the true intentions of any sport he pursued. He and his partner, Jose, cycled across the Golden Gate Bridge, but their favorite memories of that event were saved for the drinks they had later and the attention they brought on in their tight cycling shorts. What he relished most about his brief cycling phase was driving with his very expensive bike on the roof of his sputtering Volvo, until the one day he had projected that image a bit too far and pulled into the Highlands gas station unaware of the clearance he might need and tore the bike right off of his roof. He retired from cycling shortly thereafter.

I had to stop carpooling in late 2000 when I took the restaurant general manager position because of the longer hours, though I often still rideshared with Eric because he would stay late to install artwork or other distractions. My carpooling availability was further compounded by a restaurant ownership project I took on that same year with Tony and Tricia, Dominique (wine director at Sierra Mar) and Craig (executive chef at Sierra Mar). I was also doing two radio shows at the time at the local public radio station. This period was an extremely vibrant but difficult time. Eric was supportive but vocal in his concerns about my overreaching schedule and priorities. I came to suspect he created his late night projects so that we could have our car travel time, which meant our time together. It was more intimate with just the two of us, and I came to prefer it though his prominence in the group carpools was more than memorable. His group persona carpool was much more dramatic than his one-on-one with me.

My fortieth birthday party was held at his house in Carmel. He insisted it be thrown there. He had a vision. He had a fantastic plan. In the end, those who actually made it happen executed his vision to perfection, though he was conspicuously absent. He spent most of the pre-party planning and organizing vacuuming and re-vacuuming his house, although no one was allowed to actually enter that domain. The party was held outside in his yard and driveway. His OCD was making itself known, and he was using it as a cover to hide from his friends, his feelings, his fears and himself, perhaps.

The police were called twice, which gave the party legendary status for a while, and it was certainly a great venue though it would have been difficult to visualize unless it was experienced. Lights were strung everywhere, and candles flickered from every possible table or corner. The main food theme was seafood, and the spread included prawns, grilled and raw oysters, smoked salmon, halibut ceviche, crab and scallops. The seafood and sauces were paired perfectly with a variety of Alsatian and burgundy wines. People danced and laughed and told stories. Great parties have their own life force and synergy. You can plan, but you can't control. When a party becomes memorable, something magical infuses with the love, seduction and mystique, which already exists and creates something unexpected and special in the conscious and unconscious. My fortieth birthday party was that kind of party. It was great in the moment, but it became even more meaningful in memory. There was more love exchanged than I could ever have imagined.

I remember very little of him that night because he was physically absent. Toward the end of the party, he finally made an appearance. He hid until he could hide no more, and then he appeared with his mother, who was visiting from Los Angeles for the event. He had on a blue sport coat and looked incredibly handsome. I have a photo of them sitting side by side. I have a photo of them dancing. He is leading her, and she is smiling up at him in his blue jacket and black glasses. In the photo he seems to be withdrawing yet drawing attention at the same time.

When he finally came to the party, he seemed almost sad, but

I remember a look he gave me toward the end of the evening, and there was so much depth, feeling and love in that exchange I knew then, somehow, I was losing him forever. Yet, that was five years before everything came down to a single breath and hope and prayer.

Late in his illness, even though he was weak, we went to movies because we both loved matinees, and we both loved film. I was doing a weekly film review radio show at the time, and he was an eager participant in escaping to movies in the middle of the day. We had somewhat different taste in films, but we both respected high quality art design and intelligent, crisp dialogue. He had a soft spot for campy, over the top glam. He also had an affinity for stylized science fiction. He loved to bait and argue about films during carpool, and we would argue in depth about the appeal and quality of the weekly releases as well as the merits of *Star Wars*, the impact of *Blade Runner*, the point of John Waters and the demise of Woody Allen after the scandal.

I remember seeing *The Cooler* with him, something he wanted us to share. The film features William H. Macy as a down and out ex-gambler who has the unnerving ability to "cool" a winning casino table simply by sitting down at the table and touching it. When Macy's life takes a turn for the happier, his talent for cooling a table turns to making the gamblers at the table win even more money, and his Vegas bosses are not amused. Even though I enjoyed it greatly, he was bothered by the violence and said to me softly at one point, "I'm sorry." I was surprised by his words because he never apologized for anything. I rather liked it that way. We walked together for a while afterward. He was using the cane I had given him, the one I had to buy after my big-wave wipeout in Hamoa. He was talking in soft tones and looking at me with so much tenderness. When we parted, I remember watching him walk away so slowly, leaning on the cane and stopping for breaths every few steps, and I felt a small wave of comprehension rising to the surface in increments and determination. It overtook me, but I countered the awareness by convincing myself I could still change the outcome.

A few minutes later, I ran a red light in front of the Monterey police station, with a motorcycle cop right behind me, because somehow, at that very moment, I knew Eric was going to die, and there was nothing I could do about it. It was the first time my mind had absorbed that thought. It happened as slowly as a flower opening in real time photography and as quickly as a lightning bolt in a storm. And it paralyzed me. There was nothing but that overwhelming, sickening feeling of desperation and loss. I realized at that stop light, I was way beyond being able to control anything anymore. I was lost in what was coming my way, and I had no skills to guide me. I can't imagine now how alone Eric Paul must have felt. Yet, he just kept smiling with a light that was quietly diminishing while so many seemed not to notice his spirit was softly fading.

When the motorcycle cop pulled me over, he was laughing because it was such a ridiculous move on my part. He was right behind me, after all, and I was right in front of the police station. When he pulled up to my window, smiling and so jovial, he said,

"Are you okay? Are you having a bad day?"

Everything at that moment seemed so surreal I said, "Yes, I am. I just found out my friend is dying."

He stopped smiling and said some nice things, but he still gave me a ticket though he was apologetic and kind.

For the record, the last movie we saw together was *Hidalgo*, a story about the greatest long distance horse race ever run, starring Viggo Mortensen. A beautiful man riding a beautiful horse for most of the movie. Eric loved it.

Eric Paul went to Barcelona in the autumn of 2003 with Jose. He was so sick when he left that those who knew him best tried to talk him out of it for the sake of his health. He was coughing so heavily and violently by then he would often vomit in a small bag he kept with him at all times. He was extremely embarrassed by it, but there was nothing else to do except deal with the reality of his body exhuming what it needed most. The trip defined yet nearly killed him. He came home close to death. We found out later his oxygen level was at an incredibly dangerous level. After his return from Spain, he downplayed the cough and his illness for days after until he finally drove himself to the ER at Community Hospital in Monterey late one night and was admitted for nearly a week.

The few of us who could see him then had to be garbed head to toe in a body shell and facial mask. His doctors at the time thought maybe he had caught a foreign virus that was highly contagious. It was ridiculous but part of the process. We would come out of the room, sweaty from the heavy barriers required, lines on our face from masks which we couldn't breathe behind, and wonder what the hell was going on. The best thing that came out of his near-death exposure was an admission to a very credible AIDS clinic and new doctors who finally understood his lung condition and treated him with respect and meds that ultimately began to make a difference.

Before he left on the Spain trip with Jose, when he couldn't breathe without throwing up, his pulmonary doctor told him simply and with judgment, "I don't know what you want me to do because there is nothing I can at this point."

Still, he ended up going to Barcelona, throwing up in his portable Ziplocks, absorbing as much art as he could and sleeping through most of it while he encouraged Jose to go out and bring it home to him. At the end of the day, Jose would tell Eric Paul about the museums he went to without him, and Eric would relish in the details and find enormous joy in seeing the art through his partner's eyes. Jose didn't want to go without him, but knew he was giving Eric Paul the Barcelona art experience he so wanted. We thought when we finally got him back from intensive care there would be a reprieve. We had seven months. Numbers matter.

After his week in intensive care, I was present for all that he allowed me to see and more than he knew of which I was aware. I willed myself not to escape. We talked to each other every day but there was an urgency now, an intimacy usually preserved for lovers founded on whispers and hopes and shared dreams. When he was home from the hospital, I brought him food on the sly because he hated being treated like someone who needed something. But he accepted it on the casual basis it was brought and we sat together and talked and mostly listened to the words that weren't said while he pretended to eat. He would feign an excuse after a while, and I would hear him getting sick, and he then would return to our venue and we both pretended nothing had happened.

There were several bouts of hospital visits after Barcelona, but the last one was sure and swift and determined. Lung surgery, new meds, clergymen coming to call. He never talked in specifics until the last few weeks. He held my hand constantly when I was next to him. He touched my hair and told me he had always wanted to do that. We talked about my next car. He had a lot of advice. One of the things he told me was to wear more color. I smiled and listened. Every time I left his room I looked at him and touched my heart, and he did the same. Mostly, we looked through each other and didn't talk at all, and I finally and surely came to see all of him, every part he was able to give and I was able to reach. It was everything I had sensed and more than I could ever have comprehended or imagined. He was courage and dignity, personified. He was love, absolute and pure.

When he was still able to talk in that final week, a nurse came in to do something requiring me to leave the room for a few minutes. He was well-loved by the intensive care staff by that point. I still have the list of hospital workers he had me send flowers. He would whisper their names to me and make sure I had the information correct. He was adamant in controlling what little was left to him. As I was leaving the room, I heard the nurse ask in the cozy, intimate tone nurses use for patients they feel a special connection to, "So, who was that?"

"That is my closest friend," he said in between breaths so difficult to reach.

I turned and looked at him, taken aback and lost. But then found. He smiled and looked right through me in a way I had never seen before.

I swear I never knew. I swear I never. Knew.

Years later, I realized I had seen that look before when he said to me so directly when I first met him, "I see you."

And he had and did, and eventually, I him. For the ages.

PART TWO

AFTER SAL

For every action there is an equal
and opposite reaction.

Newton's Third Law of Physics

DEAD SQUIRREL HOW SAD

Christmas Redefined

THE HOLIDAYS HAPPENED. They always do whether you want them to or not. The holidays of 2006 were my first Christmas in my Carmel cottage, and since I was hosting this year, my family flew in from their various ports. Mom and Deb flew in from Phoenix, and Seth flew up from Los Angeles. Even though I had hosted Christmas several times when I lived with Alix on Skyline Forest in Monterey, this was my family's first Christmas in Carmel. It was also my first Christmas not being with Alix. I had been living in Carmel since January. It was a new venue and a different slant on traditions steeped deeply on my fifteen years of being in a relationship and my four decades of being with my family. The surprising thing about this Christmas was the liberating, loving feeling of newness and possibilities. Everything I hoped for and wanted for this Christmas came true. It was completely different. It was entirely new and intimate and filled with a new sense of love. Everyone in the family felt it as well. It felt more like a Christmas adventure. We walked the beach and took photos at sunset. We shopped together at the Carmel Plaza and had lunch downtown. We went to Christmas Eve service at the Wayfarer Church just five blocks from my cottage. We had a fire every night in the fireplace, and the mood was just light and festive and cozy. The Christmas felt as charming as Carmel.

The cottage had a great deal to do with the sense of quaint newness, but Sasha made all the difference. In every way possible, in every way conceivable, he was the cornerstone Zen. He was Buddha in orange and white cat fur. He was the most gracious four-legged holiday host, and in spite of my yearnings to "enjoy the season," I managed to stress out frantically beforehand. He watched with amused indifference, growing suspicion and mild speculation. I should have known he would have it completely under control.

My brother, Seth, has a cat named Tigre, which he brought to that first Christmas in Carmel. Tigre is shy and a bit backward for Sasha's standards though Tigre made a huge impression on all of the humans with her sweet disposition. Cats are territorial and often don't tolerate having a strange cat in their space. Sasha never had one territorial, questioning, assertive moment with Tigre. Again, he was the consummate host. My favorite image of the two of them during that holiday visit was Sasha swatting Tigre's butt in a "come on let's play" kind of folly. Tigre never played, but Sasha enjoyed himself thoroughly.

When we played the board game "Catopoly" as a family, Sasha laid himself out on the board halfway through the game, covering all of the pieces, and, I believe, claimed a protest to the capitalization of cat revenue and gain. The game came to an eventual halt, and the family scrambled for drinks. I took a picture because protest movements should be documented, and he was so cute in his resistance. Still, his presence was so dominant, yet refined and understated, I was falling in love even more with Sasha's personality and being. He won every heart that Christmas, especially mine on an even deeper level. His interactions with my family were affectionate, humorous and well-intentioned. I always knew he was exceptional and different and even strange, but now I knew he was tremendously special in a way that transformed how animals and humans interact. And love.

Every Small Thing

Sal had left in November, and within months of his departure, Sasha continued to change and evolve. His behavior changed so abruptly every day brought a new notice or revelation. He went from bad behavior to classic feline almost over night. The kitchen counters, stove and table, which he perused so adamantly before, now never seemed to interest him. His eating, which used to be based on speed eating competitions, now became refined and selected. He quit eating raw food completely. He just didn't want any part of it. Maybe it reminded him of Sal or maybe his maturity and ownership of the house changed his taste. I will never know. The rambunctious, house wrecking soul that he was now seemed to claim ownership of protecting all that he used to destroy.

Seemingly overnight, he became a gay man with refined tastes, as welcomed as it was received; it was also startling in the suddenness of its appearance. I would come home late from work and stand in the kitchen, every item in place and clean, and marvel at the quiet repose. There was no cat hair anywhere, and nothing was knocked over or askew. In the absence of chaos, I would sip a glass of wine and watch him looking at me. His chocolate smile welcomed intimacy and trust, but it also held some kind of humorous slant. As vocal as he could be, he always seemed to be in a world entirely his alone, yet also mine. He would be pulling me in and giving me distance at the same time. And I began to realize he was not slow or regressed. He was remarkable and amazing, and he was blossoming like a flower on the far side of the moon. In so many ways, he was Eric Paul.

The Weight of Him

My mother came for her annual visit in the spring. We planted flowers and shared space for a few weeks. Her favorite time while I worked, and even possibly during her entire visit, were her naps with Sasha. She relished them mostly, I believe, because he was such a good naptime buddy.

Sash always slept on my chest when he lay down with me, and

he did so with the people he most trusted. He kept that number to a minimum, which made it all the more special. Having him sprawled out on your chest like a sleeping baby was magical. He slept with abandon and love. I never wanted to break the moment, so I didn't sleep as well, but I treasured it all the same. I wasn't sleeping very well during that time, anyway (when under the duress of heartbreak, sleep and appetite are the first to abandon me), but I learned quite a bit from him about complete surrender and letting go. I seem to always have someone in my life who can fall asleep in an instant, while I struggle just to find some sense of resting. Now it seems to be a cat rubbing it in my face but with no real intention of malice or remise. As he would lie on me while I read or tried to sleep, I came to realize there is nothing much better than complete, chocolate-lipped abandon, weightless and trusting, rising with your every breath.

Sasha Speak

Sasha saying "hello" has been confirmed by several people now. My mother was the most taken and shaken of those who have witnessed Sasha speak.

One day during her visit I was in the kitchen making lunch. The water was running, so I couldn't hear very well, but I managed to hear my mom yell, "Did you say something?"

"No, I'm washing dishes."

"I thought you said 'hello,' and I'm thinking to myself, 'Who in the world is she talking to?'"

"No, I didn't say anything. Maybe it was Sasha."

And then, on cue, Sasha walked from the bedroom into the living room and said hello to my mother.

"Oh, my God. Is that Sasha? Did that cat just say 'hello?' My God, that sounded like 'hello.' Did that cat just talk? Did you hear that? That sounded like 'hello.'"

It was entertaining when people heard his words, not only because of their reaction, but also because he seemed particular about who he chose to hear them, and anyone who heard them carried on like they had never heard a cat speak before. I have read that some cats can make sounds that mimic words. Yet, Sasha had more than one standard "word." He also made a sound when he was getting reprimanded or not getting his way that sounded eerily like "no" with a look that reflected the negative. He also said "mom," or so it appeared, in a long drawn out way. Again, witnesses can confirm. I don't want to be known as "the woman with the talking cat," so I never drew attention to Sasha-speak before. Now, though, I realize how well chosen those sounds were from him.

Dead Squirrel How Sad

Driving to work this morning, I noticed, a block from my house, a large, seemingly beautiful, dead squirrel on the road. I really like squirrels, and in my head I heard myself say, "Oh, dead squirrel, how sad." I drove to work and came home to Sasha eleven hours later. It was a warm, balmy summer night, unlike what is considered normal weather this time of year. I let Sasha out when I came home, did some things around the house and then called my brother, Seth, to talk. I am the oldest of my siblings, and Seth is the youngest with ten and a half years between us. We have always been exceptionally close, especially when we were young. I remember running home after my piano lesson on the day he was brought home from the hospital, and he seemed the closest thing to a miracle my ten-and-a-half-year-old brain could imagine. Knowing and loving him from his first moments here, I have always felt a strong responsibility to protect him. I consider him one of the most important relationships in my life and even though we don't talk as regularly as we used to because of our work schedules and life interrupting, our phone talks are often long, engaging, intense and always interesting.

The sun had just set, and orange hues across my yard were fading to amber, then grey and, finally, crimson-black. I was watching for Sasha to let him in but was also engrossed in my phone call to my brother. At some point, I took the conversation outside and was standing on my porch talking. It was almost dark now, and I felt Sasha around me. I was glad he was at the house but something seemed strange. He was writhing and coddling and making strange love to something at my feet. He seemed pumped up proud and kept looking at me for approval in between his rubbing and licking and weird amorous longings for what he was engaging in so completely. Even in the darkness, I could tell he was smiling. He seemed so happy to have presented, what was now becoming evident, a dead object. I looked down in the semi-darkness and realized the object he was making weird love to was the dead squirrel I had seen over twelve hours ago. It was so stiff it could have been an exhibit at a natural history museum.

I screamed slightly into the phone, then explained the predicament. Seth tried to talk me down and gave great advice (being a film editor, he saw the humor in the scene, yet he is also an animal lover and wanted to help), but I hung up shortly after and tried to deal with the situation hands-on. Sasha, meanwhile, was continuing the post-mortem love fest and finding my hysteria more and more confusing. He kept looking to me for adulation, yet all I was giving him was my intense phobia and verbalizing it in random surges of disgust.

"Oh geez, oh my God, oh Sasha, that is gross. Okay, Sash, stop rolling in it. Oh Sasha, stop it now. Okay, that is so disgusting, Sasha, but yes, good boy, and what a good job to bring it to me. Very good job, Sash. Okay, that is really offensive, Sash. Stop rolling. Really freaking me out here, Sasha. Really grossed out, Sash. This is not your kill. I saw it this morning. You are not fooling me, by any means."

My repulsion to the dead squirrel was infused with the need not to make him feel bad. I read you are supposed to support their hunting, but this was corpse-robbing, clear and true. So I stammered, like an auctioneer wooing a bid, between encouragement and condemnation.

I hate dead things; I hate all dead things, specifically dead animals. Having Sal for nearly a year and constantly being surprised and grossed out by dead, headless mice, rats and other inanimate objects I couldn't completely identify has left me a bit jumpy and paranoid. I still walk out my door and keep my eyes unfocused as I walk to the car because a beautiful morning can be completely ruined by a dead rodent in various poses of demise.

After my mania and disgust with Sasha's new love object, I tried to focus on a plan. I would normally have called my backup, but I have no backup anymore. In all of my intimate or close relationships, I was never the one who disposed of the dead bodies. It had always conveniently worked out that way. My new backup is new support, and I certainly didn't want to use up my chips on dead squirrels and seem like a complete fragile, incompetent wuss. I decided to put Sasha in the house and get rid of the body. Getting rid of the body is always a good thing; it is the epicenter of good plans gone wrong.

After I put Sash in the house, he stared at me on the porch through the glass door, intently watching my next move. He stared a long time because I didn't have one. He eventually got bored and went to the kitchen to eat some food. I decided, after much thought, to take the shovel from the shed and toss dead Rocky onto the street so the street sweepers could deal with him tomorrow. He was so large and heavy it took me several attempts to get him on the shovel. This was compounded by the fact that every time I looked at him, I felt so sad about his being dead and so guilty about my being grossed out I had to stop. In the end I decided to take my glasses off so I really couldn't see very well and thus cut the gross-out factor considerably and sped up the process. Again, sometimes what cannot be seen cannot hurt you or make you feel bad, especially when you are already overwhelmed with too much emotional overload. Sometimes, shutting your eyes is a very good thing because your heart is seeing for you.

Still, it took twenty minutes to get him on the shovel. Eventually, I walked beautiful, dead squirrel to the road and tossed him into the street. My shaking while I performed the slinging of Rocky was an obvious indication about how bad I felt about the act, but I didn't know what other recourse I had. He was too large to put in the trash, and it was four days until garbage pickup. I should mention the squirrels in Carmel are beautiful and I hated leaving him in the street. Yet, I convinced myself the street-sweeping crew would handle Rocky gently. I went in the house and found Sasha staring ruefully out the front windows. He had obviously been watching me. His look was an intense mixture of confusion, disappointment and disgust. I wanted to welcome him to my world but just made a mental note and went to the kitchen to pour a glass of wine.

A few hours later, I went outside to look at the stars and process the squirrel night debacle. Sasha came out with me though I had no intention initially of sharing the space. He just walked with me like he often does and sat next to me while I decompressed. And then the phone rang. I went inside to answer it and eventually took the phone call outside to resume my relish of the summer night. As soon as I stepped on the porch, I knew what an idiot I had been. Déjà vu all over again. Sasha was rubbing and purring and seemingly dancing for joy. He was writhing in ecstasy. Rocky, now more hours dead, was under my feet once again.

It felt like all my blood left my body and every rational thought with it. I picked up Sasha and put him in the house and went once more for the shovel. Getting a dead, stiff, large squirrel in a garbage bag is much worse and more difficult than just getting it on a farm tool and tossing it on the street. It made my work of a few hours ago seem like child's play. Glasses off, once again, and not letting my eyes focus helped considerably, and wearing thick work gloves made me feel more brave. "Dead squirrel, how sad" went into my trash container after thirty minutes of struggle and gagging. When I came in from the ordeal, I washed my hands several times and finished my glass of wine. I noticed Sasha in the window staring longingly toward the shed where the garbage containers are stored. He turned around slightly and gave me a look I will never forget. His sad face seemed to say, "But, I brought it for you."

THE NEW NORMAL

Hoarding the Evidence

S ASHA WAS CHANGING, AND MY WORLD was as well, but he seemed to be ahead of me on acceptance. I was still struggling with the physical pain of grief. Overtly, I gave the impression of someone who had been through a great deal of loss in the span of two years but who was coping admirably. On the surface, I was carving out a new life for myself in a new home and town while successfully managing an extremely busy world-class restaurant. And all of that was true. Beneath the surface, though, was more pain and sadness than I thought possible to carry, more pain than I thought possible to overcome. I didn't know, yet, if I could survive the pain because it was bigger than me. It always seemed to be in control despite the image I was able to present to the world on most days.

Even though I was still trying to find my way in this new life and a way out from under the grief, I found solace and comfort in Sasha owning his life in such an independent manner and style. Animals are impressive in their adaptability and seemingly carefree approach to their lives. Sasha's life outside the cottage became more of his reality. He loved being outside and began to be very verbal in his need to be there. Even though he lacked Sal's fine-tuned sensibility, he made up for it in gusto and conquest. Sal killed big things. His gifts of large headless varmints were legendary and a constant source of squeamish stress for me. Sasha hunted but was too much of a lover to go for big game. He killed small mice and moles. He hoarded them, I discovered, when it was least expected.

One fine early autumn day I came back from a swim and decided to take a journal and some *New Yorker* magazines to the beach and make an afternoon of it. I had been smelling a strange odor in the office for a while but could never identify the source, and then it seemed to disappear. As I was preparing my bag of journals and magazines for the beach, I was becoming increasingly frustrated because I was looking for a certain pen and couldn't find it. I was looking through all of my bags and pulled out my favorite purse. I have a tendency not to use the things I treasure most, especially gifts. The red Italian leather purse was a gift from Agnieszka, a connoisseur of bags, shoes and all things fashion, and I treasured it dearly. When I pulled the purse to rummage for the sacred pen, an overwhelming whiff of decay met my waylaid plans. My treasured leather was reeking of dead mice smell. I did the dead thing dance, took off my glasses and covered my nose with my shirt. Inside was a grey, long-dead mouse and gone was my Italian leather bag. Sasha was outside and nowhere to be found, so there was no one to vent my frustration and strife to.

I carefully extricated all the items from the best bag I have ever known and put it outside where the putrid odor could do less damage. I went to the beach, rallied the mood and came home a few hours later. Sasha came when called and noticed the bag outside on the porch. He looked at me and slinked then played completely innocent. He delicately sniffed the bag; his eyes went wide then looked side to side and finally at me. His eyes were reeling in guilt, but his posturing was complete denial. He tried to play the disgust card. He acted as if the stench from the bag was making him sick. After our eye contact, he ran from the bag and acted afraid, then ran back to the purse and tried to act again as if it were disgusting. He would smell it then get down low and look away and then run away a few yards and look at it again. He would then look at me with eyes that seem to say, "That is disgusting. I would never leave a dead object in something Italian."

Yet, he did, and my suspicion about this cat's true identity is even more confirmed.

Body Count

When I moved into the cottage, the back yard was waist high in weeds and debris. It was a visual metaphor for how my life felt at the time, an out of control mess with no possible relief in sight. I used to think I could tame it on my own, but after a while I realized I needed muscle and help. Almost every yard in Carmel is a fairy tale of perfection. I was extremely fortunate to have forgiving neighbors, but then none of my neighbors really existed in real time. Nearly every house on the block is a monthly or weekend diversion for the well-intentioned and interesting. All the houses around me now are rebuilt with new, somewhat large homes that take up most of their assigned lots. The exception is the house on the north side of my property, which belongs to my favorite neighbors, Lucinda and Derrek. They are accepting and kind beyond reason. In my first year here, as I was waging war with vines and weeds chest-high at times, they looked over the fence for the first time with a smile and a warm greeting and looked with what seemed to be great control and no judgment at my yard.

"Hi, how's it going?" Lucinda asked.

"Hi. Rather slow, but I haven't found any dead bodies yet." They laughed at that and a friendship was born.

As previously mentioned, my rented cottage was built in the early forties and is a simple, single-wall structure, though noble. Unlike the new homes, my house is small in comparison to my lot size, and the backyard is rather generous. Taming the overgrowth came from someone I knew from work who also runs a landscaping and yard work business. His name is Saul, and he is a saint, remedy and friend in one package. In six months he had the jungle looking like a livable space through the hard work of cutting, trimming and hauling out the overgrowth of vines, ivy and leaves. Saul trimmed low-lying branches and planted new shrubs and flowers. The centerpiece of all this change and clean up was a red tile patio he laid for me in the backyard. He hauled every twelve by twelve tile from the store to my backyard without any help or assistance and then laid them out perfectly. No small feat for my uneven, root-infested yard. He also went under the crawlspace and set traps to eliminate my rodent problem. At my request, he boarded up underneath the house so the raccoons wouldn't use it anymore as a place to sleep. Their snoring was annoying, and I worried constantly about Sasha's security with them there. Yet, Sasha seemed to have some kind of peace with them.

My friend Rachel was visiting after Sal was picked up and taken to Oakland. We were talking and having a glass of wine when she jumped up suddenly and screamed. There was a raccoon staring at us through the front door glass. She grew up in Carmel and has a history steeped in hatred for the adorable but vicious creatures that wreak havoc and death on the many beloved pets of Quaintville. Because Carmel is nestled in a forest, the raccoon attacks have historically been a problem and source of anguish for the pet-loving residents. When the attacks become excessive or extreme, the *Pine Cone*, the town paper, will run stories covering the assaults and issue warnings to residents.

We both ran to the door because Sasha was outside and obviously in peril. When we opened the door, Sasha was sitting a few feet from the raccoon, which had not left his place on the porch. They both looked at us with a surprised and confused look. The raccoon ran off, but Sasha looked at me with a look I'm beginning to know well. With a quizzical, teenage sneer, he seems to be saying, "Dude, chill."

Rachel went on to lay out story after story of untimely deaths and maiming of beloved pets brought on by the eye makeup wearing, four-legged devil coon. I had always thought raccoons were adorable, but she was serious and didn't stop the heart-wrenching stories until she thought I had come around. And I did. I went to bed that night thinking I had a better understanding of what looms dangerous in the night, a source of frustration and intrigue for me since childhood, but I had no idea, really, until it was too late. I may have killed my shadow at a young age, but I never for a moment thought it didn't exist. I simply chose not look at it closely.

Clean Hands Please

The yard was now under control and no longer threatening to devour the house, but the property needed so much work I spent as much time as I could on my days off making a home for myself. I was determined to make the yard into some kind of sanctuary. I had visions of lying in a hammock and reading a book while swaying slightly, listening to the far-off sounds of waves crashing on Carmel Beach. I soon realized sanctuaries come in stages and that my work schedule was becoming more and more of an obstacle to hammock euphoria.

One late afternoon I was feeling overwhelmed by the chores I was undertaking, and Agnieszka came by to visit. I met Agnieszka in January of 2004, when she and her then-husband were looking to move to California after a brief stint working in New Orleans at a four-star resort. Agnieszka was a friend of the Hurricane's, and she and her husband, Brad, were both hoping to work at the Post Ranch Inn, where I worked as restaurant manager. I hired her immediately for the front of the house and Brad eventually became the pastry chef. After a few years, she went to work with a local fashion designer, and through a series of situations and mishaps, we became close friends.

I was raking and cutting back ivy while Sash roamed and ran loops around the house (very fast I must say) and created diversions.

Aga had only intended to stay a few minutes, but when she saw my workload, she asked for a pair of gloves and began helping to haul out the debris. We were talking and working as the day began to turn into evening. Sasha, in his never-ending desire to show off, had somehow managed to get on the roof. He looked down on us from above and seemed absolutely jovial in his accomplishment. His euphoria lasted for a few minutes, and then, for some unknown feline reason, it turned to terror. While we were raking and bagging, he began to cry and pace nervously on the roof. Despite his tenderness and well-developed feminine side, Sasha is bravado and swashbuckling to an extreme. He has always walked like his balls were bigger than he can manage, if he had some. Even when he was quite young, I watched him walk with a swagger and strut sensibility and said to a friend visiting at the time, "I think my cat is gay."

"I think you are right," she laughed back as she watched him saunter into the kitchen.

As Sasha paced back and forth on the roof, he became more and more agitated. It wasn't like him. His normal demeanor is easy-going and carefree. He has always been a strange mix of surfer dude mentality and grand diva gone wrong. On the roof he was becoming more and more frustrated and increasingly verbal. Agnieszka finally turned to me and said, "I think we need to get him down."

I had taken off my gloves a while ago, welcoming the hard work and getting my hands dirty. She offered to climb the short distance to get him, but I knew it was an easy task and that he would more likely come to me. I climbed the ladder and put out my hands to get him. He was right there, within arm's reach. He had been whimpering and crying as though he were in mortal danger, but when I reached out my hands, he simply looked at me. He sniffed my hands, looked at the dirt on them and made a noise that seemed to indicate disgust. He walked away, apparently repulsed. I tried again, talking to him in reassuring words, coaxing him to let me help him. Again, he looked at me in shame and verbalized a rant. I looked down at Agnieszka from the ladder and said, "I think he doesn't want to come to me because my hands are dirty."

It was not the first time his fastidiousness had overcome his need for help. We laughed at the ridiculousness of the notion, and then she said, "Let me try."

Agnieszka had dropped by to see me after visiting a friend and she was impeccably dressed, which is why she asked for gloves, and why it was remarkable that she even offered to help. She climbed the ladder and called Sasha's name and he was there in an instant. He took one look at her and practically leaped into her hands, her clean, beautiful hands. She brought him down and he leaped for joy as though he had been saved from a lifetime of roof dwelling and starvation. He is a very dramatic cat. He went into the house and we looked at each other in dismay and comic confusion. She has known him since the beginning and even this gave her pause. As she laughed and put her gloves back on to finish the yard work, she simply said, "He really is your cat."

"I know," was all I could say, but what does that mean, exactly?

I have known for a while, and I know the idea is improbable, but how does one dare to speak about their cat possibly being a slightly reincarnated version of someone for whom you are still grieving? All the change in my life has somehow brought me normalcy and a center. In the center of the new normal is an orange, chocolate-grinned cat with an obsessive-compulsive disorder, a huge heart and a wicked sense of humor.

Go Fetch

Over the last several months I have been training Sash to retrieve balls of small proportion. I thought cats retrieving balls was normal since I have no reason to believe otherwise. When I mentioned his passion for the game to Lori Trew, my office manager, she looked at me with surprise and said, "Cats don't normally do that."

She has been a life-long cat certified owner and lover.

"Really? They don't do that, normally?" I asked.

"No, not at all. That is rare."

"But, he does it with great enthusiasm," I countered.

"He must really want to spend time with you," she said with a soft laugh.

I thought about our games of fetch after she walked away from our conversation. I could see Sasha's eyes during those games and how much love and excitement he brought to the process. Yet, I also realized how much I loved playing that game with him and that I usually engaged him in order to get him interested. I thought I was doing it for Sash, but a vague notion was forming inside me. He was doing it for me because I wanted it so. He was being the dog I used to think I wanted.

X Games

Never one to do anything in a small way, Sasha has found a new endeavor and an exceptionally interesting way to stick a landing. He seems to have overcome his trepidation about rooftops with a dramatic flare. Yesterday, I could not see him, but I could hear his voice. His tone reminded me a little bit of Scooby-Doo when he starts low and then goes high, as if he is saying, "Hhhhhmmmm?" I finally realized Sasha was somewhere above me and then I spotted him on top of Glowie. Glowie is the name my sister and I gave to the house next door during that first Christmas in Carmel.

The house is older than mine, having been built in 1914. It is made of stone and wood and is reminiscent of a picturesque writer's cottage, which it might have been. The roof is shingled and always full of pine needles, and it slopes very sharply on both sides from the worn brick chimney, which protrudes from the middle. One night during that first Carmel Christmas, my sister and I noticed a glow in the house, which seemed to move from room to room. No one has lived in the house for a few years, and it has been for sale for even longer. Normally houses sell fairly quickly in Carmel, but Glowie had a sad resolve, and the house didn't sell till a few years later after the housing market crashed in 2008. The glow was not visible every night, but we saw it often and then more regularly.

At first I thought this perception of Glowie might be the consequence of our heightened state of awareness brought on by several glasses of holiday cheer. That theory was disproved, however, when we saw it after Christmas Eve service, clear-eyed and noel filled. Since then, the name took, and every summer when my sister visits we talk about Glowie as the house/person/phenomenon it has become.

When I saw Sasha on top of Glowie, he was straddling the top of the roof with all four paws. The roof is so severely angled, I really don't know how he managed to climb it. He seemed to be acutely aware of his predicament, though, because his eyes were wide open, and they seemed to be looking in every direction at once but not in unison. When he would try to maneuver in any way, he would start sliding down on his stomach with each paw spread out in every direction, and then he would scamper and struggle to get back to the apex. My first reaction was fear for him and alarm because I truly thought, "This is it." There was no way he was not going to get hurt in some way. My thought was that maybe I could catch him as he fell. As I began to find a spot in Glowie's rotting fence that I could climb over or through, I heard a strange noise from Sasha. I looked up and saw him sliding down the roof on his belly, paws in all four directions, and he seemed to be immensely enjoying himself. When he would slide to nearly the end of the descent, he would scratch and paw himself back to the apex near the chimney.

"My cat is snowboarding," I said to no one, though I thought it needed to be said out loud just for my own sense of reality.

"My cat is snowboarding on the roof," and it was true.

Even with the myth of having nine lives, Sasha seems indestructible. And so it seemed.

Italy

During this transformative year of 2007, I planned a trip to Italy with my sister.

It was a life-changing experience. We spent seventeen days traveling through Milan, Tuscany, Florence and Rome. I fell in love with my life again and every single aspect of Italian living. When I was packing for the trip over the course of several days, Sasha would sit in the suitcase making the actual putting in of the clothes a very slow process. Every time I would take him out, he would eventually find a way to get back in when I had my back turned or wasn't looking. Just like his disruption to the Catopoly at Christmas, he seemed to be staging a protest to my trip. I took a photo of him because he seemed so stoic and determined in his pose.

Agnieszka stayed at my house while I was in Italy and took care of Sasha. While I fell in love with Italy, she fell in love with the country of him. She, also, is not a cat person but succumbed quickly to the charm and aura of his gregarious personality. He definitely has a way of reeling in the non-believer. He does it with such intrigue and guile; it almost seems human in intent. She sent me a selfie of the two of them, and it was obvious she was smitten, but then so was he. I'd learn later on that the first night I was gone, he stayed out very late. She'd driven around the neighborhood calling and looking for him. I never knew until later how much stress he caused her. That night, when he finally came home, she had a serious and heartfelt talk with him. She told him it was just the two of them for two weeks, and he could never stress her out like that again. The rest of their time together was a bonding vacation and it sealed her love of him forever. And it seemed to seal his for her as well.

Sasha Kiss Me

Agnieszka and Sasha have a new thing though it has been going on for a while. Still, it is now definitely a thing. I think it got more pronounced and relevant when I went to Italy. Whenever she is at the house, and on whim, she will say to Sasha, "Sasha, give me a kiss."

And in his cool style, no matter where he is, he will come to her and pucker his lips while she puckers hers, and they kiss. It is so weird, yet so him, that he would know what kissing on demand means and that he is so willing to accomodate. Aga is over the moon with her new partner in affection. Their routine is so frequent now that my routine response has become, "Ok, you two, that isn't weird at all."

The New Normal

I was healing, and silently and quietly my pain was leaving. Sasha and I had a routine. My life had a new rhythm, and it felt authentic and real for the first time in a long time. Maybe ever. On the down side, I was, unfortunately, beginning to work longer hours because the new ownership of the hotel was tightening budgets, and my responsibilities were greatly increasing. Yet, Sasha and I had an understanding about my time away. He had his space and walked his world, and I trusted him completely. Sasha's bravado and confidence made him seem untouchable. After experiencing so much loss in the span of two years, I was trusting again. I was beginning to have more fun. I was believing in forever again. I was naïve.

YOUR BOY ISN'T EATING

Your Boy Isn't Eating

I T STARTED SO SLIGHTLY IT WAS HARDLY NOTICEABLE. One Saturday evening in mid-January of 2008, Sasha left food in his bowl. The next morning he let me sleep in and didn't seem in a hurry to go outside. He looked sad, somehow, and was quiet. By Sunday evening I was worried. He didn't eat anything all day. I told him I was going to call the vet the next morning. I woke up early and made the appointment. He looked at his food and walked away and then jumped softly on the couch with great effort and lay down next to me in a position of defeat. He was so still and lifeless while I made the call. I realized, then, how serious the situation had become and how sick I feared he was.

I took him to Dr. Tom, his extraordinary vet, and stayed with him during the initial exam and then drove to work. The tests were going to take several hours. It was difficult to focus on my job, and everyone in the workplace knew how important the call from the doctor had become. When Dr. Tom finally called, his voice was soft but firm, "Your boy isn't eating. Nothing is showing up on the toxicology panels we ran, but something is definitely affecting the lining of the stomach. I think we need to do an exploratory surgery to find out what is going on."

And that was it. A few days ago Sasha was snowboarding down the rooftop of Glowie on one of his extreme adventures, and today he was going into surgery. I worked, because that is what I do, until the phone call came after the surgery.

"There was definitely inflammation and a small blockage. I want to keep him overnight, perhaps even for a few days, and monitor the progress. We will know more in the morning."

Doctor Tom was extremely kind and optimistic. He was also firm and hard to read. He was following the doctor handbook, and I took all of it as a good sign. I came home to an empty house, and the absence of him was palpable. I felt it on so many levels, but what was most difficult was the silence and the absolute emptiness of his not being there.

The next morning I went to see him. He had a huge IV wrap around his front leg, and when he saw me, his eyes lit up and his chocolate mouth did that Sasha smile, but then he looked at me very directly and took his other paw and touched the IV as it dangled. He seemed to be saying, "Look at this, it is serious, but it is not. But do you see this?"

And for the first time since he was a kitten, he seemed so vulnerable and small and in need of me. Sometimes you have a realization of moments that have consequence, and this was one of them. They told me I could sit with him for a while, and I did, but I cried while I talked to him. I was embarrassed to be crying so much, so I kept putting my head in his cage to wipe my tears and softly blow my nose. He looked at me with a mixture of confusion and empathy. He still wasn't eating, and that was what would get him home.

The staff on duty came by and spoke of him in glowing terms and accolades yet always with a sense of mystery and understanding. They also made statements like, "That cat is incredible," or "That one is special right there," and then they would smile as though they were in on a secret joke. He was very sick, but he seemed to have everyone entertained and amused. It was three days until I could take him home. He finally began eating, but Dr. Tom never could diagnose what had happened to him. It could have been poisoning or an inflammation triggered by something he ate or came across. We'll never know for certain. When he was finally home, I felt as though I had been given a second chance, a gift, because for several long days I didn't think he would be coming home.

On the Mend

I was told to keep Sasha inside for at least 10 days. I knew this was going to be the hardest part of his recovery. It was going to be much harder than giving him his medications or getting him back to a regular feeding schedule. The first few days were rather mellow and easy. He was still sore from the surgery, and he would lie on my desk chair in the front room by my desk, which faced a large oak tree, the front yard, a worn picket fence and the street, in that order. The entire front of the house has small-paned windows, and he would lie on my chair and stare out, occasionally sparking some interest in a squirrel on the tree looking in at him. After a few more days, the squirrel spotting became much more interesting, and he would stand on my desk peering out at them and having some hidden communication.

By the fifth day, he was done with recuperating and using his litter box. Nature had been his bathroom preference for a long time, and now he was becoming quite verbal in his abdication to indoor servitude. He was also becoming quite verbal about everything. On the days I worked, I only had to deal with his verbose lamenting a few hours in the morning before I drove and then a few hours in the evening. By the time I got home, he was usually resigned to his captivity. Each day, though, brought stronger indignation and frustration, and with it, a louder and louder voice from Sasha. It was torturous. It was painful. It was methodical and relentless. It would begin with the usual morning nudges and staring at my face while also practically sitting on top of it. The physical attempt at intimidation was then followed by a full feline assault of meowing scales of various tempos, timbre and tremolo. The only thing it was not was tacit. Ever.

Intermingled throughout the performance were passionate deliveries of "heelloo," drawn out long and loud. It was unnerving and weird and a bit freakish. By day eight, it was very apparent to me that Sash was winning, and the endgame was near. He had worn me down methodically and with the kind of passion and drama that could only be his. On the eighth day of his incarceration, and not having work in which to escape, I knew I would not be able to make it through the day if Sasha, the prisoner, were still inside. Late into the morning of his eighth day of captivity, I looked at his orange and white face and surrendered.

"Okay, Sash, you win. We are going to go outside together, but please stay in the yard and take it easy."

I walked to the front door and hesitated for a second, only to have him nudge my leg with his head. I opened the front door, and he was free. I thought he would sit on the porch for a while, taking in the day as he normally did, pre-surgery, before traipsing off for the day's adventure and visits, but I was wrong. He ran through the door and began running laps around the house at increasingly fast speeds. I knew he was showing off but was still concerned he could undo some of the healing the last few weeks had brought.

"Sasha, slow down. Take it easy. Please."

He stopped and stared at me with a look mixed with pride and self-righteous tenderness.

"Okay, just go slow. It's okay, just be careful. I'll be inside."

I went inside and listened to the exquisite, seemingly forgotten sound of my silent house. About twenty minutes later, I went outside to check on him though I would look for him through the windows every five or so. He wasn't in the front yard, where I had last seen him, and after calling his name a few times, I heard a familiar response. It was coming from the top of Lucinda and Derek's house on the left.

(Glowie is on the right.) Their home is two stories tall, and the roof is at a considerable height. Sasha was standing on the very peak of the roof looking down at me. I had never seen him there before, and I don't know how he even managed to scale the house to get there. His look was undeniable and said it all.

"I told you I was okay." And so he was.

ALIX

In the End... Nine Jars of Olives

L OOKING BACK, I LEFT HER IN INCREMENTS, even though I didn't
know I was, because one is always hopeful that the person you
love can love you the way you wish they could. I stayed because I
loved her. There is the staying, and there is the leaving, and both can
exist simultaneously if the conditions are right. I have learned you
can love someone deeply, truly deeply, and they you, and life can
be comfortable and complete and full, yet distinctly incomplete. If
you live with someone you were once in love with, and they only
love the comfort and friendship, you are beyond hope. And without
hope, life becomes a consequence of limitations. You are not living
the fullest life you desire. But then so few are, you justify to yourself.
You are eventually alone in your feelings. You are alone in your life.
There is no other way. Love demands to be felt and recognized, and
if it is to remain unused, you are the only one left to carry it. And if
you carry it alone, you bear the weight. You create a void to separate
yourself. You think no one notices, but you know, and that is what
eventually brings you to your knees and wakes up what has been
dormant for so long.

I suppose if you are lucky, life wakes you up with death and love
then love again. You must eventually decide on what is most significant. But when you are loved, and you love, decisions don't happen.
Life chooses for you, and you are left to manage the logistics. Do
not be fooled. You are the only one who can give yourself freedom.

I had been moving for fifty-three days. Moving is a lucid word
because it means more than just the physical displacement of objects.

Leaving a home, leaving somewhere you have lived for eighteen years, does not happen in fifty-three days. Leaving Skyline Forest and moving to Carmel does not happen in a truck ride with the back bed full of your belongings. Leaving someone you lived with for eight years and loved for fifteen does not happen in a specific time frame. It happens over a very long period. It also happens in an instant. The reality happens in a moment. I have been moving for longer than I can remember.

In the end it came down to nine jars of olives. She had her people; she is Portuguese and they function as a clan, they operate as family. They came one weekend in January to move her, and they swept through like Mary Poppins on stimulants. In one weekend they moved most of her possessions, cleaned the townhouse based on discretion and removed her soul from the space we shared. I loved her clan. I still do, but they are removed from my life now, like all of her possessions, which once filled my living and breathing space. They left the place clean. She felt it was a trade off. Carpets vacuumed and a wiped kitchen equals never having to deal with me again. Her items were moved out, and there were no remnants except for the unchosen and unwanted memorabilia strewn randomly throughout and a pantry full of food and a refrigerator full of condiments and a garden full of struggling plants and a laundry room storage space full of what was once shared. And nine jars of olives on the pantry shelf.

Nine jars of olives of every variety imaginable. Spanish, kalamata, green, pitted, onion flavored, strange olive intentions of infusions gone bad. I don't like olives and never have been able to find favor with them. In fact, I hate olives though I have been trying to like them my entire life, but in the end, I was the one left to determine their fate. I tried to be neutral about the whole thing, but in the eleventh hour, I threw most of the sealed jars away and cried softly while I tossed them in plastic string-tie garbage bags. The weight of the world it seemed. But it was only olives, after all. Or maybe not. The memorabilia left behind, the secret treasures, felt like land-mines intended to inflict hurt and distress. An itinerary from the France trip in '99, pictures of her nephews, who own a part of my heart, notes left from earlier days and later moments filled with love and anticipation and, eventually, distance. Photographs, the eternal place cards, found stuffed in bags along with a ten-year-old package of French onion dip and a crumpled package of gravy mix, probably acquired by the original renter of the apartment since it seemed to have been manufactured in the 1960's. The photographs, however, were the ultimate exclamation points, because they mattered most and hit the deepest.

Irony and sarcasm, even though she wavers in the understanding of each, was never lost on her. She has a cutting and, at times, seething sense of humor, and her discarded memorabilia were most effective in their choice and placement. Sadness and anger and guilt take a toll eventually. I had been lost in their landscape for months but finally had begun to feel and see my own eventual scenario. Seeing your own doesn't mean missing the familiar. Missing her is a weight and sadness unbearable to carry and even more impossible to navigate, without any hope of having her close. I have invested fifteen years and my heart and soul, and now there is just this menagerie of remnants and my own thoughts, which feel like sand bags of emotional debris with no hope of depositing them where they could feel less painful.

There were other fates to determine. A rusted wind chime. A stained yellow legal pad, which had carried secret messages for as long as I could remember. Dozens of seashells and rocks she had collected, now discarded. A broken arrow from the earliest days remembered with her from a song introduced that seemed so fitting. A camping stick and pieces of driftwood collected from numerous beaches and trips along the California Coast. Yet more notes and cards left for me in more plastic bags from years of tender moments and soft good-byes and sweet good-mornings. Anger over what she chose to take for herself. Anger over what she left behind. Tears from moments that were only ours. A life lived and all of the obscure remnants, which must be determined or forgotten or packed away.

In the end, I tried to remember what matters most. The first night we were together. I had just flown in from Seattle. I had been in a wedding. I called her the night before I flew home, slightly buzzed from the aftermath of the celebration. We had been flirting for a year, even before her relationship with her live-in boyfriend ended, and for quite a while afterwards. When I called her buzzed from champagne, after a long conversation about what is no longer remembered, I told her at the last moment that I loved her. She answered softly with the same response. When I had flown out for Seattle at 6:30 in the morning days earlier, she had taken me to the airport. Her hair was curled, and she had make up on, and she was wearing gloves. Very sexy for pre-dawn, and I smiled inwardly and wondered, "What if?" When I sat at the Seattle airport ready to fly home, the "I love yous" already in place, I knew my life was about to change forever, and it felt right and exhilarating and curiously lonely at the same time. It felt good to be alone with the anticipation of something that was going to change my life. Because I knew it would. The anticipation was full of promise, destiny and barely-contained rising excitement. There was no doubt except for the when and where and how.

The first night I kissed her, after I got home from Seattle, on my balcony late in the night overlooking a bay of lights. It was a tender, passionate kiss, and she was open and willing and ready. I had cranked the heater up to deflect any noise in the apartment so my sister/roommate wouldn't hear any of the first moments, any of the tender firsts. The next day I went to her place in Pacific Grove.

"This is the dangerous dance," she said as you both started to move on her bed. I found out later it was a dangerous dance to her, but the words seemed so sexy in a different context.

Everything about her in the early context was intriguing and alluring; even later, when she had become much more than a dangerous dance, she was still operating on that premise. I saw and felt her that way for as long as I could. Yet, she was a master at the diffusion, at the masking, at the deflection. She was also the genuine thing. She was caring and compassionate and extremely thoughtful. She had a kindness that was unwavering. She was loving in a way that was incredibly intimate despite her vague distance, which always seemed like the third person in the relationship. She made me laugh every day. She taught me how to be light when I never thought I could. She eventually gave me a home, something I had not had with someone for a while, and she gave it to me in spades. I had been moving with my job for what seemed like forever until I got to Monterey. She burrowed in and for a while it felt safe and fascinating and made me wonder. In the end, it was a neutrality of affection, and it took years to crawl to the surface and realize it was never going to change.

The first years were a different dance of closeness and distance. She had been hurt. She had never been loved, really loved. I saw the potential, her potential, and sowed the seeds. I waited. It took longer than expected, but life intervenes. A car accident. Her depression. I nursed and waited. We traveled together, made dinners, ate out, watched movies and slept close together in an intimate, cuddling way and sometimes more. We were together, yet I was waiting for the realness to emerge. I waited for her to be present in the intimacy, but I began to love the intimacy and the closeness of what was pivotal and immediate in my life. I slowly gave in to a comfortable, amazing partnership. And it was often enough, and often it was not.

After the car accident, I brought her scones and coffee and went to her house and woke her softly during the worst of it and tried to be supportive. Driving to see her in any context are still some of the most anticipated moments of my life. I loved the thrill of seeing her because, even in her darkest hours, she had light and humor. And it was intoxicating. She would be in pajamas all day watching television. I would bring her groceries. I tried to coax her back to the living, and then, suddenly, she healed. And when she was healed, she opened up. Layers upon layers. She was able to love in ways I had waited for, but she was never able to really love physically, and still I waited because now there was a deeper love and intimacy. Yet, I knew by now what I wanted and desired was never going to happen, and my own cycles of depression and frustration escalated.

In the end, what is remembered is too vast yet too confined. But the specifics, which are infinite, are found in the fragments. The bed is moving profoundly while I sleep. It wakes me, and I think it is an earthquake. When I find my bearings, I wake her softly and ask her if she is okay. She told me she was having a dream about being a Russian dancer and that she was kicking with her arms crossed and legs outstretched.

I am sleeping at her house and am scheduled to do my monthly radio show in the morning at the local public station. There has been construction going on around her house for months. It is Sunday and they start with the hammering in the early morning hours. She goes to the window and talks to them. She is crying. She comes back to bed and says, "I just wanted you to be able to sleep for once."

We lie until we no longer can, and she makes a memorable Sunday breakfast, and I have a great show.

My sister, Debra, former roommate, has moved to Phoenix, and I am having extreme stress about where I am in my life and where my life is taking me. I call Alix at 3:00 a.m. because I can't sleep, and she drives over, and in her arms I find comfort and finally fall to where I need to be and have so much trouble getting to without her.

It is Christmas of 1994, and my family is celebrating this year at my house in Monterey, which I eventually share with her even though she goes home to Merced every Christmas to be with her family and we never spent a Christmas together. I am working at my rebound job in Carmel where I met her. When I get home from work, it is obvious there is stress among the tribe. Being the master of diffusion, she invites my brother and sister over to her vintage Pacific Grove house by Lovers Point the next day and bakes sugar cookies for them to decorate. Her entire kitchen is a Christmas elf cookie-decorating utopia, and my siblings, who are both artistic, are thrilled with their new diversion and purpose. She gets them high from a saved joint, and the cookies are world-class beautiful and crazy. Debra and Seth still talk about that Christmas and that day and how special it was for them and what a difference it made and how much it mattered.

And what mattered is so much. Hundreds of presents, a thousand hellos and good-byes and even more knowing looks and moments, which hold their own now that it is over.

"I picked this up for you because I thought you might like it."

"Have you heard about…?"

"Tell me about your day."

Soft words and long embraces. Long dinners with wine and loving talk. There are reasons why I stayed when the physical was so far removed. There are reasons why I eventually left when the physical was no longer a possible hope. I stayed because there was profound love from both of us for each other. I strayed because we had not been physically intimate for years and she told me to "do what I had to do." Both of us doubting that I would or could or really wanted to step outside our comfort zone. I had been slowly falling away from my life and the lack of a complete existence for so long that it took the crash of a huge wave to wake me. It took an intimacy I always knew could exist. It took something I always believed was possibly waiting. Even though the wave left as quickly as it came, there was no going back. And that reality was painfully regrettable yet sadly freeing.

I thought we could take it apart as slowly and delicately as it was created. I tried to make it so. The breakup took ten months, and even though we were living somewhat separate lives by then, there was talk and understanding amidst the anger and distance. There were nights when the talk and comfort level was so close and intimate I had to remember why we were leaving each other. There were also nights when I understood completely. We were still living together, which, I'm sure, to most of our friends seemed strange and possibly worrisome. After being paralyzed with indecision and fear in regard to moving out on my own for almost a year, Tricia and Agnieszka took it upon themselves, in the first week of December, to get some listings for housing rentals.

In the last week of November 1995, when Alix was gone for the weekend to a family get together/escape, it rained the entire weekend, seemingly walls of water pouring down constantly. The weather was foreboding, matching my mood and the overall feeling in the quiet, empty house. I sat in the third floor of the loft in our Skyline town-house and watched a violent rainstorm for two days. Sitting in the loft and watching the rain through the two-story windows, which looked out over the Monterey Bay, I finally let myself feel all of it. I let myself feel every single thing I had been feeling this past year but also all of the emotions I had been trying not to feel for a long time. It began with a soft whimper, and then the torrent of feelings and tears quickly matched the downpour of rain streaming down the large windows. I cried for hours over the loss of my life and the loss of love. I cried for the ending and gave it a name and moment. I let myself mourn for all of it, though I was reluctant to give in completely because I never want to lose control that deeply, but I had no choice. I lost it.

I let everything go, completely and quietly and at physical expense. It was unusual for me, but I also mourned for my pain and the toll it was taking on my entire being. I think it is the first time in my life I felt like I needed to be there for myself. The emotions and reality of the situation were so overwhelming on such a deep level. There was no one who could navigate the complexity and intensity of what I was feeling even though I had support and love. There was no magic fix. I was alone with my situation and myself. While watching the rainstorm, I knew I was the only one who could save myself.

When I finally stopped crying, there was a huge release and awakening. I felt like I was breaking out of a cocoon of long-term comfort filled with long-term boundaries and limitations. I knew I had to move on and put an end to the worst year of my life and the best years I had known. I had to find the courage to leave and somehow begin again.

After the rainstorm weekend in November, I willed myself to find a new life and home for myself. The listings from Tricia and Agnieszka were extremely helpful. A second house I looked at in Carmel already had sixty applicants, but the owner had grown up in Big Sur, and he liked that I worked there. Alix had actually gone and looked at the cottage for me because I was at work, and we both knew the house would lease very quickly. She called me when she saw it and said quietly, "It's perfect for you."

Alix knew Carmel well as she had lived there with a previous boyfriend before we became something more than friends. She and her mom loved walking the town and checking out houses. They especially enjoyed walking up to houses and looking in the windows and checking out their yards and gardens. Alix revered houses and had a special sense of knowing when someplace was special, and I trusted her completely. After she gave me the green light, I pursued the house on Lincoln Street with more determination. Moving forward felt like walking through mud. It was difficult to get traction and any momentum at all.

She eventually found a new place to live as well. She brought me to the location before she committed to lease it to get my approval, because that is what we had done for so many years. We always discussed things and made decisions together. It was a dark winter night in the second week of December of 2005. We met at the residence, and she showed me a small, but nice, mother-in-law unit behind a main house, close to our Skyline townhouse but just inside the boundaries of Pacific Grove.

"So you will be living in PG again," I said softly.

She whispered back, "Yes, I guess so."

I tell her I think it will be ok. We are both tender with each other and emotional. The dark blackness of December frames our sadness. We both begin to cry, and then she thanks me for coming to see her new place. We share an awkward, yet intimate, embrace and then I drive away. When she comes home a few hours later, she is distant. In just a few weeks, we will not be living together anymore. The finality of an actual ending looms like a presence in the remaining weeks as we pack quietly and separately. The sense of loss is palpable and crippling. The sense of change occasionally sparks hope, but it is rare and fleeting in its optimism.

Alix had a more difficult time finding a place to live and was worried about finding a space large enough for all of her possessions. One of the reasons we procrastinated so long on finding new separate living situations was her sense of despair in what was available on the rental market. Alix hates change even more than I do. She is old-school that way, embedded deep in her Portuguese psyche. It took seven years to get her to move in with me and then only because my sister/roommate had moved to Phoenix to gain entry in an MFA program at ASU. The Skyline place was exceptional in its location, space and view of the Monterey Bay, and she realized after I lived alone there for almost a year it was now or never in terms of living together. For a while she paid rent on both locations, even though it wasn't affordable, and eventually sublet her Lovers Point apartment for several years because she didn't want to let it go.

I understood, and I knew giving up the Lovers Point apartment was difficult, so I gave her carte blanche to take over the Skyline place and make it her own. She loves collecting antiques and interesting objects. It was a passion she shared with her mom, who was notorious in her early morning pursuits of estate sales in Merced. It became a passion for us, as well, and we spent many of our days off perusing second-hand stores and antique shops in our earlier years together. She made the Skyline townhouse a proper home with her tastes and quirks and her love of old, abandoned, but newly acquired objects and furniture. I came to love her quirks and taste and objects of desire because they were a part of her, somehow, and for the longest time, they were a part of me in a distant, but distinct, way.

When she moved out in the second week of January, and her family had done the fairy sweep magic of making it happen, I went to see her on her second day in her new home after most of her tribe had gone home. I still had not discovered all of the remnants she had left behind because it was too difficult to go back to Skyline, and I had put if off for almost a week. Our lease was up at the end of January, and both of us were using that last month to deal with all of the endless fragments that are so exhausting at the end of a move. I had no idea, at that point, all of the fallout she had left for me.

Yet, when I went to see her that second day in her new space and to see her mom and sister and whoever else was there, all that was on my mind was her well-being and the desire to see her family even though I knew it would be strained. But I loved her family like my own and wanted them to know I was there for Alix. In my own naïve way, I also wanted them to be there for me, in the sense of not wanting to lose their favor. Or at least to understand why the discourse had gotten us to this point. Again, I was naïve and blinded by grief. Her sister and mother were there, and they were courteous and gracious and loving. The brief visit with Alix was uncomfortable and difficult and curt. She was distant with overtones of anger. Already many of her signature older pieces of furniture and treasures were prominently displayed in her newly painted, fresh living space. Some of the arrangements and pieces stung because of their shared importance to us and their new absence in my life. I stayed strong for what seemed like an eternity, at best twenty minutes, and then made an uneasy exit.

Her sister walked me to my car and told me I would always be family and held me in a long embrace. I loved her sister and still do. Yet, I knew I would be something different to them now. When I drove away, I was crying so hard I sounded like an animal wounded with nowhere to put or share my grief. I had to pull over because I couldn't see to drive. All I could see was Alix's face before her sister walked me to the car. It was filled with so much love and fear and anguish and defiance. It was a look I had never seen from her before. She looked like a wounded lion protecting herself in a small space with absolute fire in her eyes. The cold defiance mixed with love and anger broke all of the façade of strength I had mustered for the visit. A deep part of me, my muscle memory, wanted her back, wanted the comfort zone back, wanted our life back. Yet, somewhere deep within the pain, I knew I couldn't. It was too late for either of us.

I had cried for weeks earlier because I didn't want to leave my Skyline view and the home we shared. I cried for so very long because I didn't want to leave her. I cried alone an entire rainy weekend in November that last year, while she was gone visiting family, because I knew in the end what matters most will no longer be. I cried for the futility and emptiness of it all. I cried because it was my life. I cried for the years. I cried for all of it. And then I just knew there was nothing left to mourn. You can only cry so long and then there are no more tears except in the dark moments when you have to concede.

On the last day I left the place we had shared in Skyline Forest. On the last day I had with her in our home, when all of my belongings had been moved that day and I was physically and emotionally spent, I went to her in her bedroom, her cave of escape, to say good-bye. Her bedroom contained all of her most sacred treasures, the ones I knew so well yet never felt completely connected to because they were her secrets. Even though I spent years looking at them and wondering about their origins and considering why they mattered, my consideration was usually consumed while I was lying on her single mattress bed and talking about other things with her. She always slept upstairs with me until that final year, so being in her room was like going to her den of retreat. Alix loved so many random possessions. I stopped questioning a long time ago.

When I entered her room that last day, she was so present and beautiful I was taken aback. She was calm and loving and real. She gave me a present. It was a book by Proust. I felt tears sting because I knew the reference. Several years ago, in my frustration while she was talking about something I had heard many times before, I was short with her in a rare moment of being callous. I wanted more, but I never gave her the reference point or understanding of my frustration because I never wanted to share, entirely, my isolation. I didn't want to hurt her. She was talking about something I couldn't hear anymore and I said, "Have you ever read Proust?"

The look on her face made me feel like I had slapped her. I never forgave myself for the remark. I apologized immediately, but there are moments you can't take back even though you are desperate to do so and make right. It was my heart giving voice, but I usually have self-control in those moments and I never thought she had remembered it since it was a fleeting moment. And I thought I had made up for it and made the moment evaporate. A fleeting moment of angst followed by a thousand moments of love. Maybe I willed myself to believe I had made it so. Yet, when she gave me the Proust book and kissed me good-bye, it felt like the first real kiss she had given me since that first night so long ago. I said "You have never kissed me like this before. That is all I ever wanted. Tell me, again, why I am leaving?"

Even with all of the devastating sadness of the last year, this sadness was different. It was her understanding and class and empathy that made this grief different. I felt like I was breaking in half and would be broken for the rest of my life. This was the person I had been in love with and been waiting to be with for such a very long time. This was the very person I knew existed yet was held back from me for our entire relationship. On our last official joined day together, why was I getting everything I ever wanted and knew existed? For our entire relationship, it was always just outside my reach, like understanding God or the true meaning of life.

It was a long time until I could bear the pain and weight of that last moment and all that was lost and what I didn't understand yet knew. It took years to be whole again. Yet, eventually, after a long while, you are able to move and breathe and take the small steps that you have needed to take for so long. Life takes care of us eventually. Our bodies are always trying to heal. The same is true for our souls. And, especially, our hearts.

I didn't want to deal with the deconstruction, and then I did, we did, slowly in stages, and then I realized this is what is meant to be. This is where my life is heading. My sister, Debra, came and helped me through the logistics. She was there for me through the details. She helped me move that first weekend in January of 2006 and stayed with me my first few days when I was alone from my former life. She bought me a children's book called "Wanda's First Day." It is about a young witch called Wanda and her first day at school. My sister, always the teacher. Always love and humor. She was there for me during that difficult move and that depressing but encouraging first weekend in my new Carmel house, which eventually became a home.

Our first night in Carmel, with boxes strewn throughout the cottage, both of us exhausted and a downpour of rain crashing on the cottage roof, we went to Bruno's, a local market, and bought a roasted chicken and macaroni and cheese and ate it amid the boxes and clutter and possessions that are my life. She helped me decide how to lay out the cottage and how to organize the hundreds of books, a specialty of hers. We talked and worked late into the night and drank some wine. She laid down sheets of contact paper to cover the past lives of the shelves she lined. There is always the past in every new endeavor. As we worked, the rain was constant and soothing and sometimes so loud it drowned our talk and our thoughts. It became a third person in the soft conversations. I fell in love with the sound of rain on the cottage that night. It had a different sound than the rain in Skyline. The rain on the cottage roof in Carmel seemed to wrap me in warmth and comfort and trust. And unwavering expectation.

I also felt the love of my sister in a way that I have always known but don't get to realize always in the normalcy of our lives. My sister conquers structure and planning, but I love her most in an adventure. She flew in that weekend determined to be strong and efficient and supportive. And she was beyond measure. Yet, what she gave me was quiet strength and non-judgmental support and a fierce loyalty to my life. She gave me everything I needed and more. After she flew back to her life in Phoenix, the new house was empty without her, and I missed her terribly the first few nights, but her presence lingered. By then there was the recognition and realization of friends in abundance and support overwhelming and a glimmer of hope and a new life found.

Alix's temperament toward me took a turn a few months after the move. She cut me off. In her distinct way, she told me she could no longer have me in her life. She compared me to an addiction that she needed to break. She told me she needed to have me not exist. And it added a layer of truth and hurt on a bonfire of loss.

But I did exist and we did and it was. And it is no more. And neither is she. And neither am I. And sometimes you wonder why not. And sometimes you miss her so much it makes your heart race for a moment. And your eyes fill in an instant with tears that settle on your eyelashes and stay with no intention of moving until too many join the convergence and you finally wipe them away in a non-discreet motion you hope no one will notice. Including yourself. But you do and you think of her in her new life and wish you knew who she is now. You wish sometimes you could just talk to her because even though you do occasionally there is a filter from her that is too thick and skilled to ever reveal what lies beneath and what is important to her and what is true.

You wonder about the fifteen years with her. You think sometimes about those first years without her and about who you were to each other. You wonder what matters and what doesn't and contemplate what prevails. You wonder why you don't miss her and yet miss her beyond words though you understand and accept more as time passes. You understand now most of what you need to know, but still not enough sometimes in the deep silence of late night, when thoughts rise from ashes or when a simple moment spawns a deep and loving memory. And yet you don't, but you will. You find out later it will take a very long time. You will learn it will take more courage than you thought possible. You find out too late what has consequence because you finally begin to understand the eternity of love. You begin to understand the very essence of love. And the very essence of your life. And, most importantly, the love you have for yourself.

In the end.

THE UNIVERSE INTERVENES

Grace

AﬞTER SASHA'S SURGERY AND ILLNESS, after almost losing him, our relationship seemed to go to a deeper level of appreciation for each other. I realized even more what a blessing and gift he was even though his distinctive and prodigious personality could be challenging at times. I'm not sure what understanding he came to about me, but he seemed even closer and more considerate. I kept him in at night now, and he didn't seem to mind that much. He was still social in his outings; I knew from several neighbors he was much cherished in the neighborhood though I learned later how much.

A month after Sasha's surgery, in early February, I had a birthday dinner party for Agnieszka. Because my cottage is small, we kept it to about ten people and had a Mediterranean-themed dinner. Sasha made contact with everyone and hung out for a few minutes then went to the door to be let out. There were a lot of people in my small cottage, and it was noisy, so I obliged and let him out. I told him to stay close and I would see him soon.

The party was fun, and one guest lingered late. Even though I called for him, he didn't come. I was a little worried because since the surgery, I wasn't letting him out at night anymore. After his recovery and a chance for a fresh start, it seemed like a good time to have new rules and a more limited schedule in place. Until tonight, there had been no protest maneuvers on Sasha's part. The lingering guest left around midnight, and as soon as her car started, he jumped over the fence from Glowie and walked right in, talking the whole time in a sweet tone and entered like he owned the place. He did, of course, and

I smiled as he made his entrance. It was a special night with friends, and I looked up at the star-filled sky and had that wonderful feeling of a good life: a life of grace and luck and meaning. He seemed to smile at me when I came inside. He was just waiting for everyone to leave so he could own the place again and be rid of those who didn't belong. There was something so comforting in his intelligence and social grace that I just knew we would be together for a long while, and I felt so grateful for his competent, loving existence.

Stay Close

Life eventually carves out a routine based on comfort, need and function. Sasha and I had been through many stages in the past two years, but what we had now was working for both of us, and it was more than good. March of 2008 brought hard rainstorms and some scary moments in my single-wall construction cottage. We persevered through water pouring in from under the front door and tree limbs coming down in the yard and more. During the worst of the storms, Sasha would stare out the windows with a fearful yet confused look and then turn back to me with an expression of "We're ok here, right? Because I'm not so sure." When the winds got especially high, he nervously and quickly left his lookout post at the window and burrowed in with me on the couch. We weathered the storms, and it was sweet seeing him vulnerable and worried because he never appeared so. By mid-March the storms had broken and we finally had some spring-like weather.

Even though Carmel is nestled in a forest, it is also known for lush flowers, which appear seemingly everywhere throughout the town. Nearly every home displays some type of garden or flower box or wild, natural vegetation. Throughout most of the year, but especially during spring, there is diverse and rich color vibrantly filling the Carmel palette. The intense rains of March seemed to have invoked an even stronger response for spring. Within days of the rains ending, flower buds blossomed and bloomed in a dramatic and excessive appearance. When Carmel is coming to life in spring, the beauty and diversity has an energy that is palpable.

It was a Friday, and the day was Carmel-beautiful, which is a beautiful unparalleled. The sun was shining, and the air smelled like the ocean mixed with pine and floral: spring green. The picturesque charm of the town was even more enhanced after the winter rains. The day felt like there had been a shift. Winter still lingered, but there was a hint of newness in the air. The renewal of spring was just a few weeks away.

Sash went out in the morning and came back a few hours later. I had a few appointments and was going to leave him in for the afternoon because I was going to be gone for four hours, and since his surgery I worried about losing him or compromising his safety. He pulled all the Sasha moves and acted out in a way I hadn't seen since his surgical incarceration. Through excessive pacing and extreme verbal protests, he put up a strong counter-resistance for an hour. I finally relented. It was a gorgeous day, and I hated for him to be cooped up inside all afternoon. I let him out, and as he was walking out the door, I said softly, "Stay close, ok?"

He turned his head and looked at me with his chocolate mouth and seemed to grin a "thank you." I went to my appointments and came home around five. The fog had rolled in overtaking the sunshine from earlier, and with it a sense of gloom and heaviness. I called for Sasha, but he didn't show right away, and I was tired. My work schedule had been spiraling with longer hours and more pressures. I felt a little guilty for being happy to have the place to myself but settled in for a day-off nap straight away. I dozed off on the couch and woke up thirty minutes later because I thought I heard something. I called his name for a few minutes then went back to the couch and slept another half hour.

When I woke at six, I had a strange feeling. I called for him for a while then walked the block calling his name. Something felt off. I couldn't explain it, but it gave me a bad feeling even though I told myself I was just being paranoid. This was Sasha, after all; he had overcome so much in the last few months, and for his entire life, he had always tried to make his own hours and schedule. I made dinner and kept an eye out for his return. By eight o'clock I was becoming very anxious; it wasn't like him not to come when I called for him this late. We had new rules, now, and he knew them. I couldn't shake the bad feeling, which was growing more menacing as the hours passed. I called Agnieszka and told her what was going on, and she offered to come and help look for him. She was at the house by nine, and we combed the area on foot and, then later, in the car calling his name as we drove around the neighborhood several times.

After three hours of calling and listening and looking, we had a glass of wine and went outside to talk about the possibilities. It was midnight, but we were both wired from the search and the stress. I was extremely worried, but knowing Sasha's history of self-reliance and strength, I had a strong glimmer of hope that he was okay and just off on a grand adventure. Yet, it didn't make sense because he doesn't really do grand adventures anymore. He was more of a "stay in the neighborhood" kind of cat now, since the surgery.

At one point when Agnieszka and I were standing on the porch under what had become a miserable March night, she looked at me and said softly, "I think I heard something."

We both stopped talking and listened and called his name and stood quiet. We never heard anything, though we stayed quiet for quite a while willing and hoping to hear Sasha's distinct voice. We called over and over for as long as we could without being too invasive to the quiet neighborhood. Aga left around 1:00 a.m., but I stayed awake until three and kept going outside to listen and call his name and then listen again. The silence was deafening.

First Night Alone

I didn't sleep very much. I kept waking up and going to the front door expecting him to be there, chocolate mouth and mischievous smile waiting for me to let him inside. It was a long night. Saturday morning was warm and full of early spring sunshine. I woke with dread fueled by optimism and hope. Saul, my talented gardener and friend, came early to work on the yard and do his sleight of hand cleanup. I told him Sasha was missing but tried not to show how panic-stricken I was by keeping it light, with casual drama, when I told him the specifics. He offered to go under the house to check and see if he had managed to get under the crawl space. Although there is a door to the crawl space, there are also small openings, which could still provide limited access. Saul crawled through the entire space and emerged full of cobwebs but with no Sasha. Even though he had put boards over the crawl space entry the previous year, I asked him to put additional boards over the few spaces that still offered limited entry, and he boarded it up that day.

I had wanted the openings boarded up for a long time, ever since I had heard the raccoons snoring underneath the house a while ago. My landlord, whom I like tremendously, was slow to get on board, so to speak. His reasoning was that anything could dig its way under the house, if they were so inclined, but it felt good to have Saul take care of it once and for all last year. More importantly, it gave me much peace of mind that Sasha would be safe in the future. I had always worried about the raccoons, especially since Rachel's rant on how dangerous they were, even though Sasha seemed to have a truce with them. Many nights they would be snoring so loudly under the house it was bothersome and disturbing, and Sasha would look at the floorboards for a while and then give a look that seemed to say, "Are you going to do something about this? Because you need to deal with it."

After talking to Saul and helping with the crawl space venture, I went to make breakfast. I was making an omelet and thinking about the next course of action. I often find clarity and consciousness while staring into a skillet on the stove. Small pieces and essence giving way to something bigger and more important. I made the decision to stay home from work in order to look for him. The fact that I chose not to go in to the restaurant on a busy Saturday was a serious, and possibly impactful, decision, but my heart and energy was with Sasha. Nothing else really seemed to matter. I always make work the first priority, but somehow I knew finding Sasha today was crucial.

I put the omelet-making on hold and called my day manager but kept it vague, stating that I wasn't feeling well, though that prompted concern because I rarely call in sick. Staying home to look for your lost cat doesn't invoke the confidence my position requires and normally displays. I then made a phone call for additional floor coverage for the dinner service. I could make up the admin and management work tomorrow. After I made the work arrangements, I felt a pang of guilt about blowing off work and worried about not being there for my staff. I realized I was struggling with my life-long dilemma about always doing the right thing.

I have forever anguished about not showing up to where I am supposed to be or where I am needed. When I would take a sick day at school as a child, I would literally get more sick trying to decide if I should stay home or not. Since my mom worked when I was growing up, sick days were not really an option unless it absolutely had to be invoked. I would vacillate until the very last moment, with my mom in my doorway gently, and sometimes impatiently, waiting for my decision, and then finally make the decision about which reality I would forego and which one I would choose. I have always wanted to be in too many places at one time. Were people waiting on me or was I quietly waiting for them? And where was Sasha? Was he waiting on me to find him?

All of these thoughts, and many more, were running through my head when I finally stopped feeling guilty about not working and resumed making breakfast. I was standing over the stove looking at the eggs in the pan, but my mind was on Sasha and what I should do to try to find him. I was staring at the omelet that was forming, but my mind and heart were on him and a plan of action because that is what I do in my work. I fix things and solve problems.

And that is when I heard him. It was as clear as if he were next to me. His voice was beyond intimate and more real than the omelet in the pan or my life in that moment. I heard the most loving, the most passionate, soft voice of him seeming to say good-bye but with so much love, it took my breath away. The moment was so powerful I had a physical response of weakness as though I had been hit in the stomach. The moment was so true, I distinctly tried to deny it had happened. It was so real I forced myself not to believe. I actually doubled over while holding the spatula and tried to find my breath because the sound of his voice was so ardent and so lovingly final. I began to cry softly.

I felt him so deeply and heard his voice so intensely I had to recognize it, and all I could do in that moment was catch my breath and slow my tears. It was implausible and impossible, but it was one of the most intense feelings of love I have ever felt because it was so distinctly honest and true. It was the very essence of him in the softest, warmest tones imaginable. It was his soul. It was everything he could give. It was so intently powerful that in retrospect, I should have known, and I did. I just didn't give it a reality until much later. Yet that moment, that incredible whisper of hearing him, connected me to what had become all too familiar yet finally manageable. It also connected me to the loss of him and as devastating as that felt, I was determined that was not an option. I willed myself not to be there again. As distinct and loving as his good-bye felt, I was determined to find him. Denial is a powerful motivator and eventually a drug. And a soft voice in your ear is love, personified.

I forced down three bites of the omelet and then set about a path to find Sasha.

First Day Without Him

I did two things that Saturday when I realized the situation was severe. I called a friend who has a close relationship to a rather accomplished and renowned psychic and asked for help. This may seem strange, but it felt right at the time and proved to be reassuring and fruitful. She called back within the hour and told me her psychic friend said Sasha was underneath a house in a crawl space and that if he could get to me he would. The psychic also said he loved me very much and that I needed to know that more than I realized. She felt sure if he could get back to me he would by Monday, but after that it would be too late.

At that point I went on the Internet to learn how to look for a lost cat. There are many postings regarding this issue and I was determined to learn every aspect of cat recovery. I learned several important issues: for example, after you call your pet's name, make sure you listen very hard for a response. It is also very important to post your pet's name and pertinent information on flyers and then make sure you take them down when your pet is found. I thought that portion of the program was optimistic but took hope in such success stories.

I also learned to look in gutters and small spaces as they could, apparently, wash out to sea if left to their own devices. This didn't seem right to me, yet I spent much of that Saturday and days after walking the streets calling his name and listening closely. I especially searched out and tried to find as many crawl spaces close to my house that had eluded me previously. My initial feeling was the same as the psychic's. I felt he was in a crawl space somewhere. The searching was heart-wrenching and difficult. It was also therapeutic and addictive. Yet, every session of looking for him ended in silence and rejection and more feelings of loss. I tried to be optimistic and strong, but I was so increasingly worried and sad. Just to ensure thoroughness, I also spent many cumulative hours checking storm drains and gutters and calling his name and listening, of course, because that is what the Internet said to do.

Saturday turned into Sunday with no results. I couldn't avoid another day of work and went in to the restaurant on Sunday. Aga came by and searched for several hours that day but to no avail. When I came home Sunday night, I spent several hours looking for Sasha and tried to be positive. Sal had come back after being missing for several days, so Sasha would as well. By the time Sunday turned into early morning, I let myself feel how serious the situation had become. It was a very difficult night.

Monday – Day Three

I went to work and handled as much as I could, but I couldn't get my mind off of him and the how and why and where. Lori Trew, my office manager and dear friend and a lover of cats, finally looked at me mid-afternoon and said, "You need to go look for Sasha."

So I left work early and received a negative email an hour later from the general manager of the resort. Yet, when you work ten hours, minimum, a day, I realized you can get self-righteous about small infractions, and I did with him that evening. I gave him a very clear picture of the quality of my work, the excessive hours I work and how seriously I take my responsibilities at the restaurant and resort. I also explained to him how important this particular situation was to me and that he needed to understand. In my conversation with my manager, I tried to walk a fine line between not displaying my mounting panic and anxiety over a cat while still emphasizing that I was making finding Sasha the most important thing in my life for the time being. For the first time in a couple of years, I felt overwhelmed by desperation and fear of an unknown outcome.

Aga helped me look for him that afternoon and night. We walked a huge area in the neighborhood and ended up in a house under construction a few blocks away. We called his name and both heard something at the same time. We looked at each other and thought we had found him. It was a distinct voice that sounded like him. We called the police who sent a traffic officer to enter the house. After hours of looking into the construction site, we had no answers and no Sasha. It was strange because we both distinctly heard a faint cry at the same time. We went home, eventually, and had some wine and called his name into the night, but to no avail. I was able to sleep that night, but my dreams were lonely and despairing and fateful. And sadly, remotely familiar.

The Internet Does Not Know Everything

The next weeks were filled with flyers posted and ads in newspapers and walking the neighborhood constantly calling Sasha's name. This was what the Internet said to do, so I engaged completely. The Internet said to make sure you listen after you call their name. I did this religiously. The Internet said cats that are hurt would hide until they can come out, so it is important to look everywhere and really listen. I listened and walked and listened until I couldn't anymore.

Agnieszka and I put considerable thought into which photo to use of Sasha for the flyer and missing cat ad in the *Pine Cone* newspaper. We finally decided on the photo of him standing in my suitcase when I was trying to pack for Italy. The Internet said to make sure you take down the posters after you found your cat. I relished the taking down of the posters. I worked my full schedule but made finding him my cause and purpose for being. One week into his disappearance, I found myself in my front room office looking into the front yard just wishing him to come home. I said over and over, "Just please come home, Sasha. Just please come home. Please."

I started to cry, which I had not let myself do very much since he had gone, because I just wanted to see his swagger self and chocolate grin coming down the sidewalk. But I never did.

GREENLAND

Y FIRST MEMORY OF HIM IS DISTINCT AND VIVID. We were living in Pittsburgh, Pennsylvania. It was the early sixties. I was only a few years old. He was still in the midst of a seven-year stint with the Air Force. He was stationed at the IAP Air Reserve Air Force base, and my mother and Debra, my baby sister, and I were living there with him. We lived within walking distance of the municipal airport. We were a younger, smaller version of a family, which would eventually grow to six and then, suddenly, one day be reduced to five. Every Sunday he would walk to the airport to buy a Sunday paper, and when I was old enough, around two years of age, he would carry me on his shoulders and take me on his weekly pilgrimage. He was happy then. At least on Sundays he was happy, and he would hoist me on his shoulders and talk to me about where we were going and what we were going to see.

I knew him first. He was the first man in my life, but you can never be completely sure about the moments only vaguely remembered when you are young even though they are imprinted vividly in your mind. He was stationed in Greenland while my mother was pregnant with me. Greenland is easy to remember because all of his pictures from there are white. White as the snow and icecaps he was surrounded by for nearly a year. Iceland is green. Greenland is white. I realized that at a young age even though I never learned the dichotomies for myself until I was older and could understand deeply how two separate realities could exist as a whole. It is a fundamental basis of life. It was the foundation of my parents' marriage. I grew up learning to bridge division.

When I was older and looking at his photographs of Greenland, he was a dark-haired, handsome, mostly non-smiling figure in his grey Air Force uniform in a land so white it seems as though he is in a void of nothingness. Most of the photos are black and white, and he seems surprisingly small in contrast to the stark, vast emptiness around him. As a child, this struck me as unusual and strange because he was such a dominant figure in my life. His presence with the family and in the home was omnipotent, dominant and foreboding most of the time. Still, there is something powerful and slightly haunting about the photographs. He appears both at peace and also restless in the void, almost as though he were the haunted one and had finally found a landscape suited to his persona. The rugged ice and snow softened him slightly. In the photos, he often appears to be trying too hard to be the man in the photo. He rarely seems at ease in the role of himself. He looks solitary and alone while enveloped by rugged, white harshness.

He had a passion for photography. He pursued documenting his life and his family's life through photography during the sixties and seventies when using a camera meant knowing certain things about the art form and the technology. For most of his young adult life, he photographed constantly the memorable moments and the constant change in our lives. We were always struggling financially, though my parents provided a solid middle class upbringing and life, but their arguments about money were always the background white noise of the house. Looking back, the photography was most likely an economic indulgence.

He mostly shot slides on a vintage Argus camera, and those slides reveal a remarkable and compelling story. He captured my youth and the young lives of my siblings. He captured his marriage in the various degrees of happiness and then pronounced decline. There are pictures of us through those years that reveal the essence of a family in duress but also a family struggling to find happiness and sometimes accomplishing it. His slides endure long after his presence, but maybe they are one and the same.

There are hundreds and hundreds of photos; each one is a time capsule. Each one is a memory and moment of time locked in place with his eye and shutter speed. There are too many to prioritize, but most memorable are the pictures of our childhoods. The trip to Story Book Forest in Ligonier, Pennsylvania, when we were quite young, where all of the amusements are based on Mother Goose stories. My siblings and I look so determined in trying to pull a sword out of stone. The photos acquired each year when we would travel every summer to Mattawa Falls in the northeastern part of Ontario, Canada, so my dad could fish at a power plant that was known for its surplus supply of walleye and pike. There were other families who we were close to who made the trip with us, and their presence made the eighteen-hour car/camper venture worth the drudgery and effort. Still, those trips to Mattawa were some of the very best memories of my childhood and also some of the most difficult. There are photos of dance recitals and early birthdays and Christmas mornings with toys remembered and the snapshot moment of happiness associated with each gift of consequence and impact. There are photos of Easter outfits and kindergarten graduations and holiday photos with more special outfits befitting the sixties and my grandmother's indulgence in buying them.

My father had a good eye and took good photographs until he wasn't interested in documenting his life anymore, either because he didn't care or simply didn't want to be reminded. I never knew why. I'm not sure exactly what age he was when he and his camera disappeared. He just stopped being interested. When I look back on it with adult eyes, I think he feigned interest after his family was no longer something to be discovered but more of something to be endured. He believed his family held him back. I think his passion for photographing his family ended when his passion for his family waned.

In my first images and memories of my father, his passion for his life and subsequently his family was still foremost on his mind and seemingly in his heart. My father would whistle songs, often in a half singing-whistle, especially on the walk to the airport to pick up the Sunday paper. The Sunday sojourn wasn't just about getting a Sunday newspaper. It was about watching planes scream away and majestically saunter back to earth. It was about his telling me every plane that came and went and conjuring up stories about their destinations, their passengers and their histories. His stories were enthralling and so different from his usual, often somber and serious, presence. He laughed the notes of youth and optimism. It was a song that disappeared too soon. His decisions, transgressions and brooding eventually replaced and overcame any song of promise.

My father worried about the loss of his potential in life and his lack of achieving what he felt he could accomplish at a young age. His frustration about being held back rested squarely on the shoulders of the family he was obliged to provide for and had created. I think a part of him never wanted children, despite his enthusiasm in photographing our early childhood. As he grew older, in his mind his family was the obstacle to success. His own childhood had been filled with such poverty and strife and harshness. He was alone as a child, and he was alone in his adulthood. My father carried the weight of aloneness like a personality trait. There was a heaviness, desperation and sadness that surrounded him always, even when he would be trying so hard not to be that man in that picture.

I never heard him sing after my childhood ended, after his youth gave way to middle age. His choices changed the melody. Still, he made many smart decisions. He was a smart man. He skipped a grade in school, when that was unheard of in a coal mining town in western

Pennsylvania. As an adult, he was pragmatic in decision-making and firm in his resolve, even if it meant moving his family to the Midwest to pursue an executive job with a coal mining company, when his children were deeply rooted in their friendships, schools and community. It was the right decision for the outcome, which elevated his career and income, but it destroyed what was left of a functioning dysfunctional family.

Still, I was witness to his lighthearted singing, and even then I knew a part of that melody was mine alone. I knew at that young age I was seeing the best of him on Sunday mornings, and I was grateful and appreciative in the way a child can be grateful for happiness and wonder. Even then, I sensed it was a special performance, and it would not be able to sustain him or any of us. There was something about the sadness in his happiness, which seemed obvious and suspect to a young child. It felt like the transcience and safety of his happiness could change in a moment. And it always did, especially as my siblings and I grew older.

He wanted to be a pilot more than anything he knew about his life, but due to poor vision he could never pass the eye exam, and so he spent his life working in the periphery. Seven years in the Air Force, six years as a history teacher and high school coach in baseball and football, several years in safety management for corporations and then sixteen years as a civil servant in flight safety at some of the most complex air bases in the country. Summation is cruel, concise and completely incomplete. In the end a person's life is not about the marks one hits on the stage of existence. It is more about what transpires in the shadows off stage. The real living of life exists while one is waiting to hit their cues. Expectations should never be confused with reality. Life with my father always seemed to be waiting to happen. There would be spurts of hopefulness and promise and then long periods of disappointment and emotional abuse. Yet, children always want to feel they are loved. And even in the most difficult of situations, they want to believe in hope and acceptance. Children always want to believe that good will prevail.

My father made the decision to get his master's degree in order to leave teaching and pursue a career in industry with the goal of making more money. I also think he wanted a career that held more prestige and recognition. Status was always important to him, and even though he was recognized as a good teacher and coach, he felt it was beneath him somehow. When my father finished his master's program in safety management, after two years of commuting two nights a week from Pennsylvania to West Virginia University, in Morgantown, my mother organized a party to celebrate the event. One of the surprises of the celebration was my father's gift to my brother Mark because the occasion was also to celebrate his birthday, which was the same week as the graduation party. Mark was the third child and the baby for eight years, until Seth was born. Mark was the first son, and his existence seemed to trigger a substantial amount of my father's own childhood issues. My father was a man with little patience for his family and even less for Mark. He seemed to take out all of his frustrations on the child who reminded him the most of himself.

During the graduation/birthday party, my dad gave Mark a ten-speed Schwinn bike with a banana seat and monkey bars. I was happy for Mark but also a little jealous. There was nothing as special for Debra or me in the celebration. Still, it was so good to see Mark happy and bonding for a while with my father. I remembered thinking it was such a greater and grander presentation than how he usually celebrated a birthday in the family, but then I realized, even at that young age, it was my father's gift to appease and placate all of his guilt. I also believe it was one of the most genuine gestures my father ever made. I will never know for sure, but my brother's extreme surprise and happiness over his new set of wheels was memorable and touching. Mark's happiness was always infectious, and I don't think I had ever seen him happier.

For a short while, it seemed like my father had eased up a bit on how hard he was with Mark. Yet, one of the most important elements to learn about my father was the brief nature of his truces and mild temperament. Just when everything would seem to be calm, it could change in a moment. I learned at an early age to gauge his mood and react accordingly. His violent mood swings were reflected by his behavior signals as soon as he walked in the door. Surviving his temperament was essential by understanding his demeanor when he came home each evening. My father's moods and anger held my family hostage, but we became very aware and skilled at recognizing the cues of what would trigger and who was being targeted. It was usually my mother or Mark, but no one was ever out of danger.

One of the cues my father and I hit every Sunday at the Pittsburgh airport, when I was young, was the motorized horse ride, which seemed never to last long enough for the nickel it required. The ride was mesmerizing to me and I loved it. It was the highlight of the weekly outing, and I probably cried for more than the five cents' worth. I know I did and on special Sundays there was the encore ride, even though every nickel back then had a destination and purpose. To this day, I still love airports and planes and history and a quality Sunday paper. I still love the sensation of riding up and down and feeling the dizziness of circles, which complete themselves. I still love speculating about the destination of strangers and the possibilities that exist in stories outside myself. I still love dreaming and wondering about what constitutes life and what manages to pass for reality. I am still enthralled by the concept of time and the absent void yet dominance of its presence.

I am still wondering about all of it, and I suppose I always will. In my heart, my father has passed that place. He is now endless and without and beyond. Even in his death, he is still two separate realities existing as a whole. He is now either a burden to be carried or a part of my tapestry. He is both, but it is all about how the weight shifts and the textures chosen to illuminate and how everything can be and not be at the same time. It is about loss and gain and being alone with all of it. He was the master of isolation. He was also the epitome of neediness. He was the antithesis of family. He was feared and placated. He was loved from that perspective, and it followed him his entire life. It followed him until his death, and even then there was no outlet from which to navigate, except for the channels he had already chosen, carved and perfected.

Greenland is white. Iceland is green. Nothing is ever the color it should be. Life is often hidden in the shadows, and if you can somewhat understand the darkness, then the light is more illuminating eventually. I don't think he understood very much outside the vast volumes of textbooks he read constantly. Yet, in the end I realized he knew more than I imagined or expected. By then it was too late. It always is and still he placed more value on the differences than the insight. But, it means something, it means everything, to have your father talk about your siblings because you are the oldest and he is at the end of his life, and tell you his concerns and his insights and finally realize he might actually know his children. He might actually know a small portion of this aspect of his life even though he was never connected. Even though he never seemed to be there except on his own terms. Maybe it was all he ever could give and all he ever had. Maybe in the end he knew it wasn't enough. Even for him.

And that irony is so ridiculous; it keeps my tears in check but my anger a parcel left to be opened.

It is not the size of a package that matters. It is the contents and always will be.

A MISSING CAT WILL BREAK YOUR HEART... AGAIN

Everyone Has a Lost Cat Story It Seems

SASHA DISAPPEARED IN MARCH. I called his name for months at night, when I missed him most, when my heart was breaking so. In the days I wasn't working, I walked for miles and fewer miles when I was working, calling his name and wishing his return on a level of commitment that wavered between passionate obsession and intense determination. And then after three months of heart-wrenching searching and emotional upheaval, I just gave up. Completely and indescribably. I knew I needed to stop searching for him. I needed to let go. I couldn't look for him anymore. During the period of searching, I received several strange calls from people who had seen my ad in the *Pine Cone*, Carmel's savory and unique paper, or from the numerous flyers Agnieszka and I put up. Every call would initially give me a surge of adrenalized hope only to be followed, eventually, with crushing disappointment and hopelessness.

One of my more interesting phone calls was from an elderly woman living in Carmel who had also lost an orange tabby and was convinced they had been captured by someone who preyed on orange cats and was holding them captive in their garage. I imagined her as a devotee of crime show television. Yet, she was so sincere and caring and persuasive during my phone interaction, it did make me wonder for a few days. The creepiest call came from a guy who tried to mimic Sasha's voice and said he heard that sound by his house and wanted me to come over. I drove to his area and saw an orange tabby sitting on his porch and realized it was a pick-up line and cruel joke.

Orange tabby conspiracy theories aside, it was difficult to be dealing with the fringe element when all I wanted was to see him swaggering down the walkway and know he was home. All I wanted was to know he was safe. And alive.

The Slow Walk Toward Change

There is no solace to grieving. There is no magical cure to feeling better. In the course of two years, I had lost too much. I had lost more than the expected load for many people, though not as much as some. I had been hurting then was finally healing. And that slow, eventual change was surprising, remarkable and life changing. And now I had lost Sasha, my gateway, my pure love, my lightness of being. He had been the bridge to whatever measure of healing had transpired. It made no sense. It was cruel and without warning or meaning. It was a mystery with seemingly no outcome or answers. I had just paid off his surgery from three months ago, and now he was gone. Why? I tortured myself with the "why." I ran scenarios of every sort through my head. Maybe he wasn't dead, but just gone for now. Eric Paul always used to say, "Bye, for now."

Maybe Sasha was saying, "Gone for now."

Why did I only have him for two years? Why did I not bring him in when I got home that Friday night? Why had he come to my life? Why was he gone from my life? And then one night, after I had been outside late listening for him and watching the night sky, I had a moment of intense clarity. Maybe Sasha had come to me to make sure I was going to survive those two years' of loss. After Eric Paul died, I always had a feeling of being taken care of by him. There were sixty applicants ahead of me when I looked at the cottage in Carmel, yet I was chosen. I always believed he had something to do with my getting my incredible home and living in the town he loved so much. During our friendship, he was notorious for giving me strange, bizarre but unique gifts. Maybe Sasha was Eric Paul's last gift to me. Maybe they were one and the same. On a tangible level, I will probably never know for sure. But I think I do. Yet, I'm not willing to believe the gift of Sasha is gone. And that he has vanished like Eric.

It sounds like a cliché, but time does deflect and make wounds heal, even though it is such a slow and painful process in getting to a better place. But getting to a better place eventually happens, like deft magic. Life is invisible in the day to day. It is a mirage of maintaining and surviving. You wake up every day and hit your marks and try to get through, and eventually, then suddenly, the pain you have been carrying is a bit easier to shoulder. You realize, slowly yet distinctly, the burden of carrying it is gone. And you are light and breathing in a different way, and the colors of your life have changed. And you are feeling better than you have ever felt, and your life is redefined. Your life is completely new. You simply understand your life is not about loss anymore. It is about living and possibilities and hope. You realize you are a different person in a new situation, with every element of your old self still present, but in the best way possible. Deft magic. You realize after all of the hurting, maybe it is that simple. Life takes care of us when we need it most.

I was not giving up on Sasha. I was not going to believe he was gone after being with him for two years. His spirit had always been an inspiration, and his personality is a cornerstone of my new life. He is so young and healthy and enterprising. Yet, I couldn't explain where he was or why my heart was breaking so. Again.

I needed him to come home.

GEMS AND MORSELS

Iced Tea in a Whisky Shot Glass

I LOVE MY SIBLINGS, and, like most families, each relationship is unique and distinct. When I was younger, before Seth was born, there were just the three of us: Mark, Debra and I, in ascending order. It was a simpler and less complicated time not only because the merits of youth dictate so, but also because, in retrospect, the past blurs complication through the lens of time and distance. What remains is what feels true and clear.

We were living in the hills of Western Pennsylvania, and my parents were in their twenties with three young children born within three-and-a-half years of each other. They were consumed with the day-to-day of raising children and trying to provide for their family. Duke the Dalmatian was giving rides and love and eating pancakes on a good day. Living in the country on my grandparents' farm, we gave ourselves adventures by taking picnics to the woods and staking our territory. We entertained ourselves on imagination and television shows from the sixties. We put on plays and used our "make believe" to take us away from the farm, though the farm seemed like a magical place to a young child. The hills of Pennsylvania are filled with deep forests except for where the trees have been meticulously cleared to make way for large fields and pastures. In the rolling distance, small towns can be seen in the lower valleys while distant mountain ridges maintain a mysterious and masterful balance. We spent most of our days on endless outdoor adventures and intrigues. I loved the forest surrounding our small house, and my siblings and I spent countless hours of our young lives exploring and conquering that area, even though as an adult I realize we probably weren't in the extreme wild I thought we were as children.

After returning to Pennsylvania as an adult after many years away, and walking those same fields and forests, I was taken aback by how small our "forest" seemed to be, though much more of it has now been plowed under for more crop fields and forgotten. I choose to remember the vast forest for what it was to me then, which was a fantasy, an enchanted escape from reality with a homemade lunch packed by our mother making it even more special. Those forests were our domain, and we felt humbled, yet empowered, in their embrace. Looking back, it was the independence and feeling of childhood abandon that gave our time there so much power and promise.

We would play cowboys and saloon girl, based on the many western television shows we watched with my father. Debra was the saloon girl and Mark and I were the cowboys who would come in for a drink to her "bar" in the kitchen. I'm sure it was loosely based on *The Big Valley* or *Bonanza*, but the scenario always played out the same. Mark and I would belly up for a drink and Debra, saloon girl, sassy and beautiful, would serve us a shot of whisky, which was actually iced tea in a shot glass. I'm quite sure my love of iced tea emerged from those cowboy encounters. I would also play "Nancy Dickerson, White House Correspondent," which meant I would provide pretend updates about the news into a fake "microphone," which was usually a ruler. I watched the news with my father and thought Nancy Dickerson, on NBC, was intriguing and inspiring. She was a woman in a male-dominated industry, and even my young self saw something special and unique in her professional bravado. I'm sure my love of briefcases and office supplies began during those moments.

I also loved playing "insurance man," definitely based on house calls to our rural home by men trying to sell the product. Again, briefcases were a big draw for me. Briefcases symbolized strength, and I loved the thought of having one. Eventually, I had several. I think, secretly, I always wanted to be a man because, even as a young child, I realized they had all the power.

Because of the rolling hills and mountains, our house overlooked several towns in the distance, and the view always touched something in my young self. It was the first view in my childhood that made me appreciate the awe and inspiration of the physical world. It was also the first time a view of nature made me feel the potential of my life and how beautiful the world could seem, as well as how mysterious. I was also intrigued by the towns in the distance and the people who occupied the houses. What was their reality? What were their lives? How was it different than mine from my vantage point? Could I walk to that town through the woods? Why am I here and they are there? I would have the same feelings and similar questions years later when I travelled on airplanes at night.

That particular view from our house on the farm was even more striking at night with the lights of the towns in the black distance. I remember one Christmas Eve coming home from church and looking at the lights below our view. My father was standing next to me, and I said, "I love this view so much; it is so beautiful."

"It is," he replied softly.

It was the first time my father seemed to recognize me as a person and not as a child. In that moment, I understood my own actual, individualized life and that I was a person with a life beyond this view and this reality. It was the first time in my young life that I realized my life would eventually be separate from this family and my life as it is now. The thought was startling yet also powerful. Underneath all of it was an unnamed emotion that filled me with warmth on that December night. It was the feeling of promise.

Saloon Girl and Insurance Man

In July, four months after Sasha disappeared, my sister, Debra, came for her annual visit. There is something about sisters that defies words. My sister was my closest friend and then a complete stranger. The complete stranger came when we moved to Indiana, and our family seemed to disintegrate. At least my sister and I disintegrated for a few years. We reconnected over a summer job at a country club, during college, when we were both working there as servers and unofficial, unpaid management. After several careers, she is now a schoolteacher extraordinaire in Phoenix. She married after college and moved to New York with her husband. Armed with an art history degree and a French minor, my sister took a job on Madison Avenue for a company that did fast turn-around photography services for ad agencies and then sent the photos and graphics to their clients by way of bicycle messengers. It was a speed-dial photography factory with high pressure, but she does everything well and always has.

When her marriage ended, Debra moved in with me when I lived in Monterey. Six years later, she moved to Phoenix to pursue an MFA in photography but had an epiphany about film photography and the environment and decided to become a teacher instead. She has been coming back to California in the summers to see me almost every year since she left in 1996, and I treasure her visits in every way. Debra is fun, witty and smart and every moment with her counts. No one can make me laugh and feel the absurdity of life like she does. She defies rules while adhering to them strenuously. She is contradiction and normalcy. She can be simultaneously cantankerous and loving. Her unique voice grounds me and takes me places I would never venture without her insight, support and love.

Debra came to visit in July and changed the mood and my life in every way. I was dealing with the absence of Sasha, but I was not feeling much and was hiding my sadness with everyone but Agnieszka because she was missing him almost as much as I was. I had an appointment in Salinas while Debra was here and as we were coming home, we drove by the SPCA on Highway 68. As we were driving by, she said softly, "You know, we could just look at the cats and see about adopting another one. It wouldn't be about replacing Sasha, but maybe there are cats that really need to be rescued."

"I know, Deb, but Sasha is going to come home. I'm just not ready to look for another cat to replace him."

My tone was a little defensive because my family had been mentioning for a few months that maybe I would feel better if I got another cat. They knew I was sad, but they didn't know how depressed I had been since his disappearance. I tried to remind them I had never never been a cat person, but that verbiage was getting old because I was smitten and obviously, helplessly, now a cat lover. As I drove by the SPCA and didn't stop, Debra got quiet and let out a small sigh while staring out her side window. I knew if I went to the SPCA I would most likely bring a cat home, and I didn't want to betray Sasha. On the other hand, I realized, at that moment, I never want to disappoint Debra because the sister thing is forever and sometimes little sisters can bring it, especially when you least expect it. And she always has and always will. As I took a deep breath and made a U-turn to drive back, I saw my sister out of the corner of my eye shift happily in her seat and smile.

The SPCA on the Monterey Peninsula is a haven for animals. The SPCA, in general, is a compassionate, effective organization that saves thousands of animals a year. Yet, the Monterey Peninsula is an affluent area whose residents have an enthusiastic obsession with their pets. There is more money here for animals than money for food for people in some of the poorer countries of the world. I live in an area that cherishes animals and protects them passionately. Carmel residents may be the most eccentric in their passion toward dogs and cats, with more than the occasional four-legged friend being wheeled into tea at the Cypress Inn in a baby carriage, but the Peninsula's generosity and kindness toward animals sets this SPCA apart in terms of financial commitment and long-term dedication.

It was a Saturday when we pulled up to the Monterey SPCA, and all I could think of was Sasha and that he had been gone four months. He had been a rescue cat at Dr. Tom's clinic and the Hurricane had insisted on his having a home in my recently moved-into Carmel cottage. I found out much later Sasha had been through a very difficult ordeal when he was so very small and innocent. I knew he had ringworm, which was why he was being treated at Dr. Tom's clinic, but he was also severely malnourished and was suffering from mange. His demeanor and gregarious nature was never quelled by his difficult start in life. He always portrayed the wonder of life, and he seemed to share that enthusiasm with everyone he encountered.

Again, I was not interested in adopting a new cat. I was still devastated by Sasha's absence. I still missed him every day, and more nights than I am comfortable in saying I called his name into the Carmel darkness. There is something to be said for not disappointing your little sister, but as I drove into the SPCA, I was thinking about all those hours looking for Sasha on their website and on foot, and all I was feeling was the loss of him. Yet, the interesting thing I learned about the SPCA is that it is truly difficult to be sad while you are there. The Monterey County facility is newly built, and there are many open areas for animals to run and play. Even though the animals have cages, the pens are generous in space and very clean. Although it is an animal shelter, it feels more like a temporary good home for an animal to find a guardian. There is even a wooden cutout of animals where you can have your picture taken as you stick your head into what would be their face. My sister and I couldn't resist and took a photo with our faces squeezed into the various forms. She was a cat on a fence, and my face was attached to a grey dog on his hind legs with his paws up, either ready for a treat or a double handshake.

When we parked at the SPCA, we were immediately overcome with righteous rescuing. Still, all I could feel was Sasha and the love in my heart for him. When we got out of the car to enter the SPCA, I said to Debra, "I am not getting a new cat. I still don't know about Sasha and where he is."

"It's okay," she said. "We are just going to look. It will be fun. Let's just do this."

I couldn't deny that it would be fun to look at animals with my favorite person and sister of my life. I also couldn't deny that the entire scenario felt strangely familiar. There is always hope at the beginning of anything of consequence.

GREENLAND REDUX

THE MORNING MY FATHER DIED I was alone in my cottage in Carmel. Debra, Seth and I had been with my father just a few days earlier, for almost a week, in Panama City, Florida. He had been struggling with myeloma for several years. I knew when we left him at the end of that visit I would not see him again. I knew there would be no more family visits to Panama City even though there had been only two. One with Debra and one with Seth. A few years separated those memorable, difficult, yet profound, visits. For a long time, I felt guilty for not visiting him more. Even when he was living in Atwater, California, working at Castle Air Force Base for a few years, an assignment he chose because he would be close to his children, since Debra and I were only two hours away and Seth was six hours being in Los Angeles, I saw him only a few times. The visits felt forced, like he was trying to make up for lost time and be the person in the photograph he had been before he became the person he is now, and also make up for everything else that had transpired in between the two exposures.

On one of those visits to Merced, I remember looking at the bath towels and realizing they were the same ones from when he was still with my mother, many years ago. They were ratty and old, and I felt slightly embarrassed of his resistance to change. I also felt appalled at his frugality and inability to create something better for himself. My father was always frugal with his money, time and emotions.

He used to tell us a story of when he had a paper route when he was young, and he would hide his hard-earned money in his mouth because his older brothers would beat on him until they got his coins. He felt putting the coins in his mouth gave him an edge if he could just hold the coins in for the duration of the abuse. He told the story like a funny anecdote, but he always seemed sad when he talked about it. And after hearing the story a few times, I realized, even more, how alone and difficult my father's childhood had been. Sometimes, that realization made me sympathetic for brief moments during his flashes of anger, long bouts of silence or distance. Eventually, no amount of sympathy or insight could bridge the discord and disappointment.

His apartment, during those visits, smelled like cigarettes and the past. There was always the faint smell of dust and sadness. I knew he was making all of the effort, but I was aloof with him in a tender way. I'm sure it didn't feel tender to him. Even when I was doing it, I felt sorry for him. I knew I should be more forgiving. I knew I should overlook his opinionated comments and his strange way of trying to connect with me through video games, which featured attractive women playing poker. I knew I should overlook all of his stammering attempts to make things better. I knew in my heart I should embrace his attempts to be closer to us. I knew I should be kinder to him. And I wish I had. I was a younger version of myself, then, and the immediate past weighed in much heavier at the time. Sometimes, memories dictate what can be done in the present. The past that matters and remains always paves a way for the determined future. Even when we try to forget and forgive, we sometimes simply can't forge a new path. Even when we know we should.

My father eventually gave up on his children and California. I think he realized we were never going to let him into our lives or forgive him for the life we had with him as children. As for California, he hated how high the taxes were and how liberal the state leaned, in general. After only a few years at Castle Air Force Base, he put in for a transfer to Tyndall Air Force Base in Panama City, Florida, and received a substantial promotion and increased responsibilities. In the spring of 1992 he came by to see Debra and me on his drive and move to Panama City and stayed for the night. It was bittersweet and awkward. Having tried his best to be more involved in our lives, and not having his efforts reciprocated, his demeanor during the visit vacillated from aloof kindness to sarcasm to veiled anger and resentment. In a way, I couldn't blame him.

He talked about the move to Florida. He chose to live there because they don't pay any state sales taxes. He was excited about the move and seemed anxious to put California behind him, and that seemed to include his children. When he drove away the next morning in his Ford Mustang, I felt sorry for him in his aloneness. I felt sorry for him in his sadness. I felt sorry for the loss of effort and time. I also felt incredibly sad for the loss of him. When I watched his car drive away from Skyline Forest, I knew he felt rebuked in his attempts to be a better father and make up for his mistakes. Even though I gave him more time, I never let him feel close to me. And even though I felt guilty for it, I still couldn't love him the way he needed or wanted. I wasn't sure sure anyone could, but then he met Jean.

My father loved living in Florida. He loved the sunshine and status. He bought a condo, settled in to his new position at Tyndall and reinvented himself. He started a new life. In August of his first hurricane season, he met Jean as they waited out the wrath of Hurricane Andrew at their condos in the complex where they both lived. Jean was a blonde, attractive woman a few years older than my father. She loved to cook and was extremely conscientious about her health and lifestyle. My father, a safety management expert, kept her safe and calm during the fierce storm. They were never apart after the storm settled.

Jean saw the best in my father because that is what he presented. She was proud of being a southern, genteel woman with fierce beliefs in the Republican Party and the Baptist Church, but not necessarily in that order. She fussed with a nervous energy my father seemed to overlook while she took care of his every need. He was from that generation, after all, where wives doted and catered to their husband's every whim. Jean was docile and attentive but had a steely resolve and deep commitment to her beliefs. She was also rather affluent. For my father, it must have seemed like the complete package.

I kept a journal that last week at the hospital with him and my siblings while we kept watch over his final days. In fact, my father asked me a few times what I was writing and not in the most inviting of ways. I told him I was keeping a journal about my visit. He made a disdainful face and then did his infamous scowl. Jean, always overly optimistic, said, "Jack, Wanda is writing short stories. She is going to write a short story about this someday." It was a nice gesture on her part since I had no idea what I would be writing about in the future.

He stared at me for a notable pause then looked away. Because of his medication, this exact scenario and Jean's exact words repeated on a continual loop for several days. In a few versions, my father is muttering to himself as he turns and looks away. I surprised myself by finding humor in the continuous loop of "Wanda, what are you writing?" and my father's varied responses to my reply. He never reacted the same way twice, but it was always with various degrees of suspicion and distrust.

When I reread the journal, years later, the entries ended before the final goodbye. Even though the journal has hundreds of specific moments, my last words to my father exist only in my memory. I never finished the journal. When I said goodbye to him at the hospital, I tried to pretend this was not my ending with my father. I tried not to feel that absolute and yet still understand it on some conscious level. When I said goodbye to him, I knew I needed to convey everything I could feel into that moment. I looked into his eyes and held his hand.

I told him I loved him. It was intimate, yet vague and wanting.

In the immediate years after my father died, I meant to fill in the journal with those last moments, but I never could. I couldn't bring myself to write those last pages. I remember the look in his eyes. I remember his voice when he told me goodbye and that he loved me. It was meaningful and personal. Yet, like my first impressions and moments on Sundays and the mechanical horse ride at the Pittsburgh airport, they are blurred yet specific. What I remember most about my last moments with my father is telling him goodbye while trying to remember all of him and making the moment mean everything it could. And trying so hard to make it right. After one take and leaving the room, I went back to make the second take better. Neither one seemed complete in what I was feeling or seemed to mark the moment for what it was or should be. Later, when I was trying to understand why I felt disappointed about that last moment with my father, I realized I was hoping for a movie ending. I was secretly hoping, perhaps, that a magical movie-moment ending could change the previous reels. And then, I also realized there are no retakes.

Still, those last moments with my father are mine and ours, together. He looked me in the eye, and even though he seemed a bit out of focus because of his medication, the connection was more meaningful than I had ever felt before. I know those last moments to be true, but even as I was leaving the room, he was immediately focused on the nurse in the room and on trying to get more comfortable. He was complaining about how his pillows were not propped properly. I know I was not an afterthought, but his attention was already somewhere else. He was talking to the nurse about how uncomfortable he was as soon as I let go of his hand. I saw him completely, but I will never know what he saw or felt in me. And that is the final memory I took with me as I walked away from my father for the last time.

I flew back to California and resumed my life. I kept in contact with Jean through phone calls and tried not to feel guilty about not being at the hospital anymore. I was also trying to not feel guilty about being relieved to not be at the hospital anymore. It was good to be back in the semblance of my own routine and life. On the morning of May 4th of 2006, I was sleeping deep after working a long day previously at the restaurant trying to catch up on work from being away. I had gone to bed late because of my extended day and had been having trouble sleeping because I was worried about my father's condition and just worrying, in general. The sound of knocking woke me early in the morning. I tried to ignore the constant disruption because I was in a deep dream and was fighting coming to the surface. When I finally focused in on the sound, I realized it was coming from my window. I became aware it was a bird pecking insistently at my window. When I was more fully awake a few minutes later, I opened the curtains to find where the pecking was coming from and saw a bird fly away. After I thought about the moment, I realized I should call Jean.

I reached her on her cell at the hospital, and she told me my father was taking his last breaths. Even though my father's health had been deteriorating rapidly, I was still stunned to learn he was actually about to die. Jean seemed excited that I called at that moment. She seemed relieved to have someone there with her. She sounded exhausted but also intense in the situation. As tired and numb as I was, I listened to my father's last breaths as Jean eagerly put the phone next to his mouth. I was uncomfortable with this reckoning, but I knew it was important and forced myself completely out of the last remnants of sleep to be present. I listened to the intermittent sounds of my father's breath while Jean infused comments about how close he was to dying. It felt strangely as if she were calling the scene for me like the play-by-play at a sporting event, even though I was an unwitting participant. Her nervousness and sadness seemed to succumb to a sense of urgency, and I could tell she took the communicating of his breaths seriously.

As I sat on my bed on a sunny May day in Carmel, I tried to imagine the scene she was describing. I tried to visualize Jean whispering into the phone while she intently followed my father's every breath. It was extremely intimate, but also surreal. Eventually, I felt privileged and grateful to be there, and my "presence" seemed to mean so much to her. At least she was not alone in the situation. After fifteen minutes or so, Jean's commentary and the slow breaths of my father finally found each other, and both were silent. Jean, as always, was stoic and matter of fact, yet there was a vulnerability I had never heard before with her.

"Your father is gone."

"Are you sure?" I asked because it still didn't seem possible. I would realize later that was the same thing I said to my father when he called years ago to tell me my brother Mark had been killed.

"Yes, he is gone."

She was much more matter of fact the second time she said the words. There was a long pause, which was filled with silenced emotion.

"I'm so sorry, Jean."

"It's just so awful, Wanda. But I'm so glad you got to hear his final breaths."

I had mixed feelings about that statement because, even though I was grateful for the moment, I was trying very hard not to be unnerved and overcome with my father's last breath in my early morning ear. I was trying very hard to do the right thing and focus on the woman who had held the phone next to my father's fading breaths and interjected commentary like she was doing a live broadcast.

"Are you okay? Is there anyone there with you?" I asked her.

"No, I need to get the nurse. There are things that need to be done."

Jean was a widow when my father met her. She was a retired nurse, and her first husband was a doctor who was one of the founders, and had been on the board, of the hospital where my father spent his last days. She always had a no-nonsense approach to handling the more sensitive and harsh things of life.

I tried to be supportive even though I was with tears and had an overwhelming mix of emotions. Even though her background of southern right-wing conservatism was often difficult to overcome, I focused on her moments of softness and her hospitality when I visited the few times I made the journey. I tried to focus on her loss above mine. I wanted to be there for her, and even though my empathy for her seemed forced at times, it was sincere. The dichotomy of two realities coexisting, yet fighting against themselves, was palpable, then recognized. I understood this dance. I was adept at the moves. Even when trying to grieve for my father, I was placating and trying to understand her situation and both sides of the coin. I heard my father's dying breaths three thousand plus miles away, and it was arduous and heart-wrenching, yet what lingers is the drama in the way the moment played out.

My father was often about drama, and Jean was drama, personified. When I was listening to my father's last breaths, all I could hear was her complete focus on his passing. Jean's fade toward lack of drama as my father's breath slowed made me feel a different connection to her and a huge compassion. I also finally realized I was hearing my father's last breaths in real time. I wanted to be there and not listening on a phone as he passed. After he was gone, I wish I could have been there for Jean. Her heartbreak was so immense it put a perspective on mine.

When I was no longer on the phone with her and could process the early morning reality, I shed tears for an undetermined amount of time but then was slowly surprised by my relief. Relief for him not being in pain anymore. Relief to be free of his pain as well. Relief in the letting go. The person known and the person not known and the sadness of that reckoning. It was such a strange sensation to be grieving a loss that had been transitioning and known and suspected for a while, yet also accepting a reality of separation and release from guilt and frustration. Even though it sounds ridiculous, I was unprepared for his death. I had thought about it, but I never accepted it actually happening.

My siblings and I flew back to Florida a few days later for the funeral. I had an early flight. Alix came to pick me up and take me to the shuttle in Monterey, which would take me to my flight out of San Jose. When I woke that morning, I had a heavy heart but was determined to give my father's funeral the very best part of me. I wanted to be there for him. I wanted to be present for all of his passing and his life. When I got out of the shower, I felt suddenly ill. I got sick to my stomach but thought maybe it was just nerves or the orange juice I had drunk on an empty stomach. When Alix took me to a coffee shop to get a pastry and a beverage, I got violently sick to my stomach. When she then took me to get my shuttle, Agnieszka came by to give me support and by that time I was feeling very ill. I had a plastic bag with me, and realized I may need to use it in case I got sick again. By the time I was on the shuttle, I was extremely ill. There were only six people in the small van, and I was in the front seat. I tried to focus and meditate on not getting sick again, but right before we reached the San Jose airport, I quietly threw up again into the plastic bag in front of complete strangers. I was mortified and ashamed. The shuttle driver was kind and indiscreet and quietly put on the air conditioning and turned it my way. I kept trying to understand if I had the flu or if it was an emotional response. I was also very stressed about how sick I was feeling with all that lay ahead. I had to get myself through two flights to reach Panama City as well as the funeral, which was scheduled for the next day.

After I was dropped off at San Jose, I raced to the bathroom and was now throwing up and having massive lower intestinal attacks. I called Alix and Aga for support, but no one could really help me. I was violently sick, and I was the only one who could deal with the situation and get myself to Florida. After we took off from San Jose, I saw one open seat available near the airplane's bathroom. I moved myself to it and then proceeded to use the bathroom nearly every fifteen minutes. I had never been this sick in my life. It was violent and without reprieve. You know you are violently ill when you are incredibly grateful for a toilet, no matter what the condition of the toilet. When you are being ill at a coffee shop or balancing yourself between both outcomes in a small cubicle of a plane, you are just thankful for an outlet. This is when you know you are the most sick you have ever been. At one point a young airline steward came and sat next to me and said sympathetically, "Are you ok?"

"No, I'm really sick, and I'm going to my father's funeral." And then I felt tears begin to roll down my cheeks and my emotions swell the way they can when a total stranger is kind to you when you need it most. I felt so extremely ill and more alone than I think I had ever been.

"I'm so sorry, let me get you some ice chips."

I was so embarrassed but so grateful. The ice chips helped tremendously, and he was so gracious and caring it nurtured my guilt and validated my quest.

I had to change planes in Memphis, and walking through the airport and smelling all of the barbecue nearly killed me. Yet, while waiting for my flight in Memphis, my body simply had nothing left to dispense, and I started to feel some relief though I was still nauseous.

By the time I arrived in Panama City, I was exhausted. Jean had booked my siblings and me into hotel rooms. Deb and Seth went to a dinner for the family, but I was still too weak and ill to go. Two of my father's brothers had driven down from Pennsylvania for the funeral, and another brother had come from Georgia. All of them had made the trip for the service, and their tender love and support made all the difference. While everyone was at the dinner, I ordered a grilled cheese with fries from room service, one of my favorite comfort foods, and watched television while reveling in my small comfort of beginning to feel well.

Again, I have never been that ill in my entire life. Was I purging my father? Was I feeling the stress of losing him? Did I have the flu? I was just starting to come to terms with feeling better when Debra rushed into the hotel room, visibly upset, and told me about her evening. Jean was dictating the terms of the funeral and didn't want Seth to read my father's favorite poem. Jean was always hard on my sister because Debra wasn't about bridging alternate views. She didn't silence when she was suppose to acquiesce. I've always loved and admired that about her. She has always been about speaking her truth, even when those of us around her knew it would not end well, especially with my father and now with his wife. Jean never found southern favor in challenging the norm or truth. Jean was always about maintaining the status quo and her view of what constituted her reality.

My father loved the poem "High Flight," and Seth wanted to read it at the funeral, but Jean had her own vision of my father, and we were a disruption to that existence. ("High Flight" was also the poem television stations used as they signed off with airplanes soaring back when television stations actually used to have an ending to their broadcast day.) Deb had stood up to her and there was a tempestuous showdown. My uncles were on the side of my siblings, and Jean eventually acquiesced, but it made for a stressful night for everyone. In the end, Seth read the poem beautifully in the midst of a very religious Baptist funeral.

During the outdoor funeral in the marsh of Florida, the people who spoke about my father only knew a small portion of him. They knew his later years. They knew him in small divots and portions. The minister talked about a Baptist army coming to take everyone. We were raised in a compassionate Christian church, which was quite far from the rhetoric being spewed at the funeral. I kept wondering during the service how my father ended up in a Baptist army and why this army seemed to matter so much to him. The same minister came to see my father during one of the last days my siblings and I were at the hospital and spoke then, as well, about the army of Baptist rebels trying to take back the world and the perished souls. My father was so infatuated with his rhetoric that we had to leave because it was so disturbing and outside what I thought was my father's religious perspective. But my father's religious rhetoric changed often throughout his life.

My father's funeral was organized down to the finest detail by his wife, yet I'm sure they talked on some level about what he wanted. The extreme right-wing rhetoric couldn't just be coming from Jean. Still, it was isolating and challenging to accept. I tried not to listen closely to very much of it. At one point, I looked out over the expanse of the serene Florida cemetery and landscape and thought I saw my father. I know I felt him. He seemed to be smiling. The tropical setting was a long way from the coal mines of Western Pennsylvania. I think he was proud of that somehow. Everything surrounding him was surreal except for his presence, yet he was beyond reproach. At one point in my non-listening I saw several cranes grazing in the distance. They were magnificent in their silent presence.

During one of the last days at the hospital, before my siblings and I flew out to our other worlds, my father had a moment in the hospital. Jean was doting over him, but he was uneasy and frustrated. In the turn of five minutes, he went from being loving with her to spewing profanity and extreme anger toward her. It was severe and seemingly out of nowhere. It was a combination of his medication and his latent personality. After it was over, she sat down and started crying. I had never seen her be vulnerable before that moment. My father had become a better man with her, and she had never seen that side of him.

"Why did he do that to me? Why is he acting like that?" she asked.

"I'm so sorry that happened to you. But that is my father," I said quietly. "His words don't mean he doesn't love you. He just does that sometimes."

She stiffened, then softened, and said, "He's never been like that before. He's never spoken to me like that, ever."

"I know, but that is the person I knew throughout my life, and I'm sorry you had to see that," I said quietly but with gentle conviction.

Jean always vehemently denied the portrayal of our father in the stories we told about our childhood, though it was not often discussed. I will never forget the look in her eyes after our exchange. It was as though her entire reality had just shifted, and she was trying desperately to understand who she was in her new world. Her husband was dying, but in the turn of a moment, she didn't know who he was anymore.

I'm not sure we can ever really, truly understand a person, though we may on our own conscious level be in sync with what they portray and what is perceived. We put references and thoughts into comfortable containers we can acknowledge and access and love. Knowing someone on a deep level is subjective yet biased. What lingers and is remembered is the memory and the influence. What we leave behind is how much we loved. And the difference we made.

There are three gifts that my father gave me that came completely from him to me. The presents were an anomaly because my mother always bought the presents, but these were selected by my father exclusively. There were a few others after he and my mother divorced, but the ones most notable reflect him best despite their time frame.

The first one was a chair from his mother, which he gave me when I was in need of furniture and also wanting items from my heritage. It was a vintage table chair made out of maple, which he painted black. I'm not sure why he painted it black. This was the late eighties, and I was young, and maybe he knew I was into black kitchen items. Still, he was so proud of his renovation and re-creation. It is a great chair, but the black made the history disappear and all of the past. He was extremely pleased with his efforts in sanding and then painting it the color he thought I would like. His lengthy story about his refurbishment seemed at odds with the outcome. Still, I thanked him profusely, but the chair seemed distressed and out of place, and the black only emphasized more the disparity. I had heritage through the chair with a grandmother who was distant though caring in an aloof way. She was a grandmother who was not enamored with children, even to the point of not wanting them to be present at Christmas, but at least I had heritage. My paternal grandmother softened as I grew older. She seemed to like the grown-up version of who I was, and eventually I saw her in a new way. Yet, the chair carried a dark remembrance of the whispered politics and discretion of my father's family. It also made me realize how far he had come.

The second gift was a toolbox that I asked for one Christmas because I was on my own now and felt I needed a toolbox filled with what I thought I needed for my new world of independence. This was during my "I can fix things" stage, though I had no idea how to fix anything. And I still don't really. This was after my parents' divorce. This was when Christmas got complicated. This was when

I thought a toolbox could amend my life and give me answers. He gave a feminine version of a toolbox in a pastel color with a few tools inside the box. I suppose he thought I would fill it eventually with what I needed. What I needed was for him to give me the tools that would sustain my life and explain them to me. I never had that input from him, but I filled the box throughout the years in various ways. I often still don't have the right tool for the minor "fix-it" projects I attempt. And honestly, though I have fixed very few household jobs, when I do, I am filled with immense independent pride.

In this sense, I am much like my father who attempted throughout his life with our family to be a fix and repair kind of guy. Unfortunately, his victories were few though his attempts were many. His most infamous repair and installation job had to do with the shower door in the master bathroom when we moved to Indiana. My parents gave the "larger" bedroom with its own master bathroom to Debra and me, because we were so unhappy with the move and so despondent. He attempted to replace the plastic shower door with a glass one on three different occasions. Each one broke for various reasons. The first one cracked after being installed upside down and he forced it to close. The second one broke after he kicked it "accidentally." Each failure filled the house with lament, anger, frustration and dread. The anger and frustration were from my father. The dread and lament were from everyone else.

By the third attempt, my father displayed a new attitude and approach. He was practically Zen-like in his demeanor and posture. Instead of swearing and ranting when he confronted a problem, he was calm and relaxed. It was impressive but strangely alarming. Not only was my father battling the door installation, he was also confronting his past bad behavior during many other repair and home improvement jobs. My mother and father fought often and intensely during those situations. Having grown up on a farm, my mother didn't think my father knew how to get things done properly and would offer "advice" and opinions that didn't sit well with him. Her remarks would begin with gentle insights tinged with a softly veiled, barely visible sarcasm, then matched by equally but slightly elevated benevolent, restrained responses from my father. After many back and forth passive-aggressive suggestions and retorts volleyed, a full-blown shouting match would inevitably ensue. This pattern was so familiar that, I realized years later, some part of my mother never wanted him to succeed in these endeavors. The slow progression toward the eventual fight would build with the painful swiftness yet slowness of an emerging black hole. After the explosion there was nothing but silence.

After my father installed the third door, he triumphantly announced his success and gathered a few of us to witness his accomplishment. He was like a kid with a jubilant need for redemption. When I went to see the new door, he boasted about his ability to beat the other negative outcomes.

"See, I knew I could do it. You guys didn't believe me."

At that moment, he turned around with his new power screwdriver running at high speed and accidentally touched the glass door. It shattered into a thousand pieces. I thought he was going to cry, but he just walked away, defeated it seemed, but speaking a few profanities under his breath. It was comedic pathos, but I tried not to laugh. I felt bad for him, though it was incredibly funny in a silent comedy film kind of way. He was always trying to prove himself and seek redemption. Yet, he brought bragging rights so often it was sometimes humorous to see him outside his element, which was scholarly and analytical. Outside his element, perhaps not surprisingly, his ego always led with a vibrant confidence even when the results were less than successful, even when they were disastrous. After the third glass shower door exploded, he put up a

Plexiglas door without comment except for the nondescript, "There, that is done. I hope you like the new door."

"Thanks, Dad, you did it," I replied, trying to make him feel somewhat better about the three previous failed attempts.

My father was a professional grunter, and he let go of a world-class grunt and chortle with his response, "Yeah, I did."

I still attempt small victories with tools and repairs, yet they are few and far between. I love the research and a good hardware store, and buying tools still infatuates me.

The third gift was a grey plastic piggy bank my father gave me when I was six and very sick with the flu. Even that young, I was surprised by his tenderness because it was rare to see him visibly worried about me or my siblings. I carried that piggy bank with me for a long time because of the tenderness it represented. When he gave it to me, he talked to me about the importance of work and saving money. This was before he went to college and became more of the person he wished to be in order to escape his past and a pre-determined future.

Before the G.I. Bill gave him the opportunity of a college education, my father drove a milk truck delivering all of the Sani-Dairy products to the small towns around our area in the mountains of Western Pennsylvania. This was during the early and mid-sixties, after my father finished his seven-year stint in the Air Force. He was trying desperately to find his way in life. He hated delivering milk and thought the job was beneath him. Yet, I loved when he drove the dairy truck and couldn't wait for him to get home because he usually had a treat and a fair amount of optimism in those early days. I know he felt the job was undignified because I often heard words about it between my parents, and he practically told me so the day he gave me the piggy bank.

"Just always remember, it's important to work hard. Even if you don't like what you are doing. Sometimes you have to do what you have to do to get by. I'm not always going to be driving a milk truck, but I have to do this for now because of all of you."

Even as a child I sensed his self-serving sacrifice and resentment, but I also saw a sadness in him at that moment that was touching and enclosed with love. He could never have understood that I never loved him more than those years he wore white and delivered milk and dairy products to our neighbors. I was so proud to tell people what he did for a living. To his chagrin, I bragged about it.

And, when he brought home chip dip and chocolate milk on Fridays, he was the family hero. I never felt that way about him ever again.

PART THREE

AFTER SASHA

*The speed of light within a vacuum is the same
no matter the speed at which an observer travels.*

Einstein's Theory of Relativity

HOPE DEFINED

Little One

DEBRA, EVENTUALLY, got me to the area designated for cats, and we looked at several felines. I wanted to adopt an older cat that would be easy to bond with and easy to find a quiet co-existence. Yet, every older cat was acting like a fussy older cat. I held several, but there was no connection or bond or even friendliness. After feeling frustrated for a half hour or so, I went into a different room in the cat area and noticed a small grey and black spotted, striped wonder and went over to that cage. She was so little yet determined. This cat never let go once she was on my radar. Her tiny kitten body was a beautiful mix of grey and black with white on every paw, only in various degrees of application. Each foot had a different amount of white applied and distributed. Her coat was filled with stripes and dots, giving her an exotic flair. Even in her three-month-old feline body, she was absolutely adorable while being majestically beautiful.

When I finally held her and did the "cat on their back holding test" for temperament that the Hurricane had taught me, she scored huge points. The test requires holding a cat in your arms on their back like a baby and then letting them arc backwards with their arms outstretched. Supposedly, many cats can't do this maneuver without extreme agitation. Yet, the cats that trust and enjoy this position are evidently smarter, calmer and better adjusted in their environment. I know it was true of Sasha, and this new little one just stretched and fell in a comfort zone that I, personally, had not experienced in a long while. She laid herself out under my hands and purred the kitten tones I had not heard in too long. She seemed to stretch and make herself comfortable for the long term. It was more than noticeable and hard to dismiss.

When I put her back in her cage as I was going to leave, she clung and held on for as long as she could attach herself to me. When I was finally able to get her back in the cage, she held on to the cage with her arms and legs spread wide apart and seemed to scream, "Please don't leave me here." I have a photo of that moment, with her arms and legs clinging to the cage in her desperation, and the anguish on her face. Even though I tried very hard to be objective and noncommittal, she absolutely had me at that moment.

Debra and I conferred and discussed and pondered. She was wonderful with the no-pressure sale, yet giving me the gentle, insistence tactic of "this is a great cat" scenario. I made a hasty decision to take this little one, simulating, in some respects, the same way I came to take Sasha. I trusted my instinct and listened to my heart. The way this little one cried when I was trying to leave left no doubt about her intentions to be in my life. Even though her cries and pleas not to abandon her were different than Sasha's initial cool seduction of me with his direct, calm attitude and laid back approach, the feeling was the same. This small cat chose me. Irony is difficult to deny. Her name at the SPCA was Kim.

Media Child

I went to do the paperwork to adopt "Kim," but found out she was going on television the next day to do a commercial shoot for the SPCA, and they could not guarantee an adoption. They told me I needed to be at the SPCA after the television shoot first thing in the morning, when they opened, in order to be guaranteed her adoption availability. Deb and I came home after doing the preliminary paperwork and talked about the leap of faith to adopt another cat. There is something about an object of desire being difficult to acquire that makes it even more desirable. That night, I became determined to adopt this small wonder of a kitten, and Debra and I plotted our rescue for the next day.

When we arrived early the next morning, we did the paperwork and took Kim home. The paperwork went well and was easy, even though there was always the possibility that in her cuteness she would become a media star after her television debut, and one or more of her newly established adoring fans would be in competition for her adoption. That scenario was playing out in my head though, fortunately, not in real time or reality. I worried the night before we adopted her that there would be a drove of people wanting her after starring in the television commercial. Yet, it was surprisingly easy the morning of the adoption, but I also felt we got a bit lucky. In addition to the luck, there was my sister and I making things happen, which is what we have always done, and an adorable, seemingly grateful kitten emerging into my life and space.

When the staff at SPCA put Kim in a travel box for me to bring her home, I knew something special was about to happen. I knew something life-changing was transpiring. I knew because I had had this moment before, and I knew how much adopting an animal could change your life. I wasn't sure if I were ready for anything new or different or needing my attention. I was teetering between the magic and hopefulness of new possibilities and still feeling the sadness and loss of Sasha. Dual realities and a dichotomy of feelings. The eternal conflict of loss and hope.

There is something spiritual about bringing an animal home from a shelter. It is a moment that exists only one time. It is a moment that is completely defined by hope and promise. I remembered the moment I brought Sasha home and how he leaped and bounded and kitten-hopped with such abandon and glee. I remembered his absolute joy in being in a free space and making it his own. He owned his space immediately through sheer happiness and an innocent love that was palpable in its exuberance and huge presence.

Kim did not disappoint. She hopped and rubbed her scent on everything available. Walls, stools, furniture, carpet, nothing escaped her need to be everywhere in the cottage. I wondered if she could smell Sasha's scent and was trying to make the cottage her own space. At one point she rolled in what could be described as a kitten somersault. It was heartwarming and special, and I enjoyed it immensely, but Sasha was in the room and in my heart. It was bittersweet. Love abounded with every kitten-hop and a sense of renewed expectation existed in every bounce and movement. It was a life moment. Still, the shadow of Sasha was so strong for me and still so sad that I felt him strongly the entire night of Sophie's first night at her new home. It didn't diminish the joy, but I felt him even more deeply. Where was he now? I had looked for him for four months. Why did I not have answers? His unknown was present every moment of my day. His absence was my baseline. And his unknown was my unknown. Every day was an effort to begin again without him. The definition of loss.

Debra and I debated and discussed names for Kim at length and after a night of deliberation, I told Deb I wanted to name her Sophie. It kept the "S" theme intact, and Debra agreed: she was, indeed, a Sophie. Her sophistication with the photo shoot and commercial sealed the deal. It was a good first night home.

Sophie's homecoming was also special because Debra was here to share it, and Agnieszka also came by later to share in the kitten joy. The newly proclaimed Sophie was putting on a show and reveling in the attention, and we were reveling in her newfound love and acceptance. Alix came by later to visit my sister (they have known each other for nearly two decades and have been close at times throughout the years) and fell into the Sophie "adorable kitten watch" as well, which was a rare thing since Alix is not an avid animal/pet lover, though I believe that has softened in recent years. Alix dated someone for several years after our breakup, and he had a dog, which she came to adore. We were all so fixated on Sophie's first night home and her happiness and kitten joy that relationship boundaries and division just fell away. There was no past history or hurt in the room that night. There was just love and acceptance. Sophie redefined social structure the first night she was with me. I was impressed with her early influence and relished my luck in finding her. As much as I was missing Sasha, this new little one was dashing and charming. I couldn't wait to see how it played out with Sasha when he got home.

Houston, We Have A Problem

The morning after we brought Sophie home I checked her litter box and saw blood. Deb was just waking up, and I said, "Houston, we have a problem. There is blood in the litter box." (My sister is an aficionado of movie lines and I couldn't resist the urge to use the *Apollo 13* line even under such dire circumstances.)

The SPCA does such profound, prolific work, yet they rush all of the procedures in order to get the adoptees ready for new homes. Sophie had several procedures within a few days at the SPCA, which involved spaying and multiple vaccinations and such. I was hoping she was just reacting to her immediate operations and recovering. She was so fun that first day, incredibly loving and discovering and adapting. By the end of her second day home, she was sneezing and distinctly not feeling well. I called the SPCA earlier about the blood and they were upbeat and informative about the situation. They said to give it a few days and that the blood was normal. I gave it a few days, but Sophie's condition continued to get worse.

I took her to Dr. Tom, who was so compassionate with Sasha always, and he diagnosed her with kennel cough. She was sick from being exposed to other cats at the shelter. I didn't give it much pause.

He prescribed medication, and we brought her home. She was still adorable in manner and she took the meds with no trouble. Yet, she continued to get worse. I was so blessed to have my sister visiting during this time because she was such an anchor for Sophie when I had to go in to work and also when I didn't. Even with the additional support and attention for Sophie, her condition did not improve. In fact, she was getting sicker every day.

After many days of coughing and sneezing so hard that her body would shakes violently while an entire cloud of saliva and mucus particles erupted from her small mouth, I took her back to Dr. Tom. He examined her thoroughly and said softly and seriously, "This cat is really sick." He knew what I had gone through with Sasha and that he was not in my life anymore, yet not defined as to his circumstances. Tom, master of holistic medicine and professor of wisdom, said quietly, "Only you can heal this cat. Only you can heal her."

"What does that mean?" I asked him softly.

"This cat can only recover if you give her what she needs and will her to get better. She's very sick. I recommend eucalyptus baths and heavy medication, on time and with diligence. And just will her to be better, and she will."

He had such a quiet confidence that he made me believe.

I left the appointment feeling overcome with worry yet responsibility. If Sophie were going to survive, I needed to manifest the outcome. I needed to will her to live. After everything I had been through in the last few years, this was a challenge and a great opportunity to knock death in the face and still be standing. Death had been beating me up lately with little warning and utter defeat. If I could help Sophie survive, it would be a small but meaningful victory.

Steam Baths with a Kitten

Debra was truly wonderful with Sophie while she was visiting. The two of them definitely bonded and forged a relationship, even more than Sophie and I because of my work schedule. When I was at work, Debra gave Sophie her meds, showered her with love and attention and kept a very watchful eye on all of her movements, which were mostly sneezing and sleeping. When Deb had to leave and fly back to Phoenix, Sophie was still sick and not getting any better. The night before Deb flew home, I gave Sophie another eucalyptus steam bath to help clear her lungs. My sister is pure love to me. I don't see her enough or hear her witty banter nearly enough, and that is always a source of sadness for me. When I was sitting in the bathroom euca-lyptus "steam bath" with Sophie, Deb popped her head in to check on us and said, "How are you two girls doing?"

"I don't think I can ever smell eucalyptus again," I said with a sad smile.

"Hopefully, you won't have to," she said with a soft voice and smiled as she left the room.

The eucalyptus baths were an event/ordeal that I finally mastered after a few attempts. Sophie was so small, and everything was new to her, so she adapted rather well after a couple of sessions. I would draw a bath and put an excessive amount of eucalyptus oil in the water, all the while keeping the bathroom door shut in order to maintain the most steam. My forties-style cottage is special for many reasons, but holding heat, steam or warmth is not one of its better virtues. I would get the bathroom as steamy as I could, and then I would get Sophie from the living room and we would sit on the toilet lid with towels over our heads and breathe in the potent steam together.

During the first session, she seemed terrified, but eventually, it seemed to help her sneezing significantly. She was initially agitated and confused, despite my attempt to be calm, and even though she resisted a bit, she eventually breathed in the herbal air and found it soothing, but it was a struggle. After the first attempt when she was so stressed, I decided to be more of the solution and part of the process. I would create the eucalyptus bath and hold her and breathe in the steam in a dramatic fashion while she watched me as I held her in my arms. She eventually began to imitate me and would breathe long breaths through her nose, all the while looking at me for approval (or perhaps just attempting to placate my strange behavior). Yet, the eucalyptus baths became very effective, and her breathing began to be noticeably better after each session.

That last eucalyptus steam bath, before Debra had to fly back to Phoenix to begin another school year, was melancholy and sad. I was worried about not having her here to help with Sophie's progress and recovery, but I knew she had to get back to her life. Even though we had special dinners and talks and a tremendous amount of fun, much of my sister's visit, as it turned out, was about nursing Sophie's tiny body back to health. I don't think Sophie would have made it if Debra had not been here during that period, that year of importance. Much of my sister's visit was also about the love between two sisters and what can happen when the rest of the world fades away for a little while. And the hope of healing a very sick kitten.

Watching Her Fly Away

Yet, seeing Debra fly away, after the adoption and the support and the love, was more crushing and sad than it usually is when she departs. I have a thing about flying. I absolutely love every sensation about being in an airplane. I love the feeling and transformation of flying in a small cubicle that magically takes you away from yourself and your safe routine. It goes to the deepest part of me and my earliest memory with my father. I love the sensation of departing from a known place and arriving somewhere new. I love how different and whole it makes me feel. I am inherently changed when I fly from one space to another, and I know some of the wonder is not only founded in my moments with my dad and his love of airplanes and his stories, but also my fixation on time and the displacement of moments. How can we exist in one place in the present and be somewhere completely different in a matter of movements on a clock? In a matter of measured time, our complete recognized reality is changed. And how is the past present bridged with the present future except for our known recognition of understanding the experience? And what do we really understand about the experience or what time truly means?

I love flying at night and seeing the lights of towns and cities below me, like a beacon that is both a question and an answer, wrapped around me like a cocoon. I love imagining the lives within those lights. Whenever family or friends fly in, I love watching them land on arrival with shy expectation and the ginger reconnection of shared love and memories. Similarly, when they depart there is the sweet melancholy of memorable shared time mixed with the sadness of not sharing space anymore once they leave the airport terminal and my physical reality. After they are no longer in my shared space, I wonder about the realities of their life and my own and the promises of what time will bring and what their life will be after my time with them. Where does one go when they disappear? What are the walls of reality and shared time and when does it change to memory from reality? I am probably too obsessed with time for my own good. ("Too obsessed for your own good" is one of the many sayings from my grandmother's repertoire.)

Since throwing a ball against a wall when I was ten, I am still intrigued with time and what it means while we pass through its corridors and how we navigate through our lives while knowing we will eventually be in an absence of time. Even when I was young, visits with my grandmother or close friends would begin to turn to anxiety the moment when I realized I was going to have to eventually say goodbye. At that moment, the thought of saying goodbye and leaving was so overwhelming it often ruined what was left of the time remaining. Looking back at my young self, the thought of losing love and being without the people who mattered most in my heart severely affected my ability to love in the moment. I eventually outgrew this quandary, but it remains a light shadow deep within me.

All I know is when Debra departed, and I watched her plane soar towards Phoenix, I felt alone and profoundly sad and scared. I watched the plane till I couldn't see it anymore. I knew my mom was waiting for her in Phoenix. I knew with accuracy what her night would be like, but I also knew how empty my evening would be without her. We had yet another close and wonderful summer visit. I watched until there was nothing left to see, and then I drove home to Sophie and this new responsibility and life.

AN EMPTY BOTTLE
OF ABUNDANCE

M Y SISTER LEFT ON TUESDAY. It was now Saturday, and I can still feel her on the couch knitting the Fair Isle sweater she was working on. I can still see her alternating between one of the several books she was reading and watching one of the high-definition channels on my television. She had never watched high-def before, and she was hooked, like a junkie who finds a drug of choice, finally, after experimenting with so many bad options. Her eyes would glaze over while she watched a nature documentary on Nat Geo, smiling slightly, her stare intent but aloof. (I remember that look on my father's face when we got our first color television.) Sibling happiness is important, and there are few comparable feelings of contentment as when you can make that happen, even if it is with better living through television.

She was here nineteen days in July but not nearly long enough. Everything is different and yet nothing will be for long. It is a theme that rises every day, like the occasional brief sunlight battling another foggy summer in Carmel and settles in for the long stay. Her absence speaks to me at night, when the waves are crashing, blocks from my house, and the night feels closer than it ever has. I look at the sky late at night and look for her in the dark, silent stillness. I miss her. I miss Sasha.

When I went back to work after taking a week off with her at the end of her visit, schedules, invoices, payroll, employee reviews, reservation requests, budget submissions and hundreds of emails were waiting for me. Life goes and goes and goes. It ebbs and flows.

There is loss and gain and frustration and joy. There are all of the messes that make the fabric, which makes the art. And the art is undefined and loosely held.

I didn't notice until several hours into the first day, when I was still missing my sister so much, that someone had put a glass jar in my inbox in my shared work office. Considering the office I share with the executive chef is not much bigger than a broom closet located in the back of the kitchen directly adjacent to the small employee bathroom and directly in front of the prep station where the proteins are broken down, I was surprised I hadn't noticed it. I am often looking for distractions from the odors and equipment noise outside our open office door. It was a beautiful jar. It looked like an old milk jar from my childhood. It was perfectly clear and clean and empty, but on its side was the word "abundance."

When I took it out of my inbox, I thought someone had left it there as a joke or with good intention on giving me levity on my return to the reality of work. For several days I tried to find out who had put it in my box and asked people, "Okay, who left an empty bottle of abundance in my inbox?"

I asked for a week, and no one knew anything about it. After a while, I quit asking and simply would look at it for minutes on end, pondering the possibilities and the implications. An empty bottle of abundance. It defines everything, and yet answers none of the questions. Yet, it parallels my entire existence before my sister reached my doorstep. When Sasha went missing, it brought back so much of the heartache that I had finally moved past in the last two years. With Sasha's sudden absence and loss, I fell into a low-grade depression and high-level sadness. There were mornings when I couldn't get out of bed. I would never admit that to anyone. But those mornings, when there seemed to be absolutely no point in anything, are all I can remember before Debra arrived. The grief and sadness consumed everything, and yet I kept it out of sight. I hid it from my staff at work, and I hid it from my friends. The stark realities I keep to myself. Always.

I only get my sister for three months out of the year. Because she is a schoolteacher, she spends all of her days and nights working toward the outward goal of making a difference. She would hate my calling that obsessive dedication. All I know is that after the bell rings in August, I rarely get to talk to her until the bell rings again late in May. This is my reality with her. Throughout the year she is constantly grading papers, preparing lesson plans and dealing with student/parent issues. She hates talking on the phone, so our conversations, when I get them, are short and succinct. She is always working from home after her days of working in the classroom. She performs all of this mayhem and constructed march toward hopeful excellence with the backdrop of a few "must see" television shows in the background. My sister is highly proficient at multi-tasking. She is highly proficient at everything she sets her sights on. She doesn't know this, but I do because I have been watching it all my life. After sibling rivalry subsides, there is just admiration and complete awe.

When my sister was going through her divorce, she moved from New York and was living with me in Monterey. She decided she needed a diversion and set upon learning to weave and spin wool. She decided to learn Swedish in order to go to that country and spin with a native. She never made it to Sweden, but she taught herself a fair amount of Swedish one summer a few years ago. She lived with me for five years, after her divorce from her best friend, husband and love. I would come home from work, and she would be spinning and carding the wool and smoking. She could spin wool and smoke and never lose a beat. It was hypnotic and mesmerizing. She was laying her goods out to dry and laying her heart out with every stroke. It was an agonizing gift to receive.

"SHE SLAYS DRAGONS...
IN WOOL AND COTTON AND FIBERS"

I want to see that on a billboard. I want to buy a billboard for my sister with that message screaming across the universe because she would never consider it, and the message is too true not to acknowledge.

Debra's yearly summer visits often develop theme catchphrases based on occurrences or transpired events, and this year was no exception. We listened to Johnny Cash, and I have had "It Ain't Me, Babe" in my head for at least two weeks. Not the movie version, with Joaquin Phoenix and Reese Witherspoon, but the really annoying bad version with Johnny, himself, and June Carter. I still hear the dated trumpet staccatos over the words, "No, no, no," and the painful pause before they say, "Babe," so flat and angry. I have been wondering if you can go insane from a song playing over and over in your head. Or worse, from just the same lines echoed over and over. Or worse still, combining those lines with "I still miss someone," which I do constantly, both in my head with the music, but mostly in my heart, which has been silent for so long. I am quite sure the insanity question will play out sooner than expected.

The scratching noises in my bathroom had started again. They are either raccoons or wood rats or unnatural nocturnal evildoers, depending on my fear level at the time. With Sasha gone and his hunting prowess unchecked, the scratcher elements have gained an advantage. My sister heard the scratching when she first came in early July, but it went away until now, several weeks after her departure. I need to open the closet where I saw the mother mouse and her four slimy babies two months ago. I am sure they had left through the hole the mother had created. That was a very memorable Sunday night for me. I truly hate rodents, and I really hate being alone when I have to deal with these kinds of distressing issues. Being alone is not for sissies. I never really understood that until a while ago. When my sister was here, I moved the two traps my friend Christian had set in the closet. They never went "whack" in there like he predicted and longed for, but that only seemed to prove my theory of the little slimy family being gone.

With my sister here, I felt a surge of rodent confidence and moved one trap to the garage and one underneath the house. It took a week of checking the traps to finally have any activity, but I did come to really enjoy the anticipation. Deb would say to me occasionally, "Have you checked the traps today?"

I came eventually to love the responsibility of checking the traps. It made me feel like I was living in Alaska or some wildly independent state of being. Finally and ironically on the same day the one under the house was flipped over but empty, and the one in the garage had a dead, grey, lifeless form in it.

My sister said she was not squeamish and offered to get the little grey one out from underneath the table where he lay trapped and bent. I never knew she was not squeamish, so I was quite pleased at her offer.

"Are you sure you are ok to do this?" I asked, impressed but skeptical.

"I'm good to go," she said imitating Jodi Foster in *Contact*.

All I had to do was hold the garbage bag, which I did quite expertly, until either she or I jumped upon pickup, and my sister ended up throwing the mouse and trap at me. Fortunately, it landed in the bag after bouncing off my arm. It was sheer reflex and timing. All those years of sports still pay off when you least expect it.

Headless creatures are difficult to deal with, and dead things, in general, give me a bad case of the shivers and elicit utter disgust. I learned to deal with the disposing of dead rodents by various means. The most effective was taking off my glasses, so I really couldn't see very much, and waiting until dark, so visibility was quite poor, and dealing with all of it with a garbage bag and a prayer. I was forced to learn that technique out of necessity because of the extreme hunting skills of Sal and Sasha. It made me realize, though, I have a difficult time looking at death and the physical reality of dead objects. Maybe it is empathy. Maybe it is the hardcore connection. When Mark died, and there was a closed casket, all I wanted was to see him, even in his mangled state. I wanted to touch his leg or some part of his body to know he was really in that coffin. I wanted to know that he was really gone because I couldn't believe that he was not living anymore. I couldn't believe he was dead. I didn't understand how one moment took him away.

I drove my sister to the airport. We arrived early. She wanted it so. My sister hates to fly, and even though she seldom shows her anxiety, transporting her body through the air in a small vessel makes her noticeably uncomfortable. There was a big to-do about her baggage because she was worried about additional charges, but her weight was to the pound. I knew it would be because she weighed herself with her baggage three times to make sure it wasn't over the limit. She packed for five hours the night before between sister talk, glasses of wine, the high-def distractions, and her need to have everything in her bag perfectly organized and situated.

We sat outside the airport for a while. She smoked a cigarette and told me not to cry because she couldn't and if she did she would "lose it." I was strong. I gave her the goodbye she wanted, and then I went to the observation deck and waited because there was nowhere else to go. I waited and wondered and felt the sad heaviness when love leaves. I decided to wait until she boarded the plane.

The Monterey airport is small and the airplanes smaller still, and passengers still enter by walking on the tarmac and climbing up movable steps. It was a long wait. When she walked to the plane, she turned and waved, climbed the steps and then waved again. I wanted to say, "WELCOME TO VIETNAM," one of her catchphrases during the visit from the first Saturday night she was here, when we were seduced by the Miss Universe pageant being held in Vietnam and being broadcast in HD.

The pageant people thought it wise to have a young girl scream, "Welcome to Vietnam," in English with massive enthusiasm and a heavy Asian accent. My sister mimicked it perfectly and used it while shopping, while eating and while having nondescript conversation. Usually, it was in reference to something not being made in China, but I never knew when she would belt it out, and that made it even funnier.

I shed a few tears first when she boarded the plane; small tears with no place to hide. Her plane taxied, finally, and then went down to the end of the runway. By this time, I had made my mind up to stay till the very end. I was going to watch her soar over me and then think about going home, home to an empty house, but my home nonetheless. I thought, for a moment, her plane had left in a different direction because it was out of sight for so long, but I knew better. I know the flight patterns of those leaving, even though it has taken me a while to understand.

After a long while, her plane finally soared and took flight. I knew from her boarding she was on the side of the plane where she could see me. The plane rumbled and roared and found flight and air before it reached the observation deck. I waved my arms and stepped back so she could see me. I waved until she was just a speck in the sky and let the tears fall. I felt her completely, and my life wrapped around me like a blanket. I felt completely loved and completely alone. It is the succinct dichotomy of life and the anguished outcome. In those moments, those precious moments, when you feel all that you need and all that you don't have, all you can do is surrender and embrace.

Before my sister came, I spent money on new lawn furniture and tried to make the yard look inviting. I worked on the subtle finishes that would entice her to spend an afternoon reading a book under a beautiful Carmel oak. This did not happen, and it was not her fault. The days were cold. The leaves kept falling. It was nature's version of *Groundhog Day*. Every day I swept the brick tile patio that Saul had built for me, and the next day it looked as though it never happened. She spent her days inside, soundly so, and invested in projects, the two of us and Sophie. It was perfect. I watched from the sidelines and breathed it in like air from a sacred place I can usually only admire from a distance. I never realized how alone I was until she left. I never quite understood how much I loved her until she was here and then gone. Every year I rediscover this love, and every year it is taken from me.

Why does love ever have to leave?

An empty bottle of abundance. How perfect. How defined. How unknown. How much in need. What price to fill. How strong the desire to fill it, still. The mysteries make the difference sometimes. Sasha. Mark. The mysteries help me understand, yet they make me question more. Eric Paul. Definition is always elusive. Alix. Mystery is infinite.

There are a hundred things I could write about my sister's visit. I have many of them written down on a legal pad. All of the nuances and the words worth noting and the moments captured on a daily planner are there for the reckoning. But still, nothing can and nothing will.

I miss the sound of knitting needles and the sound of my sister's voice. I miss the sound of her silence. I miss absolutely everything about her. She made me realize how much I miss my life with Sasha since he has been gone and, eventually, she made me realize how much I love the life I now live because of him. Beyond encouraging me to adopt Sophie, my sister managed to bring Sasha full circle for me and, in the process, gave me some momentum to move forward.

Despite the fears and the thin membrane between reality and imagination, I suppose everything is possible. It is mine for the taking. I just need the strength to make it so.

Memories become dreams eventually. I have learned that lesson. My imprint in this space has become part of that reality. It makes it easier, but it doesn't make it any less. My reality these past few weeks was my sister. Her absence only makes the silence and the words more real. Still, I hear… "No, no, no, it ain't me, Babe. It ain't me you're looking for…

Babe."

"And I still miss someone."

UNDER ORION'S BELT

The Beginning and End of Things

I CAME HOME TO SOPHIE after watching my sister disappear into the clouds. My focus was on Sophie now and how to make her health better while maintaining my difficult work schedule. I continued to give her the medications she needed, and I kept up with the eucalyptus baths. I gave her as much love as I could, and even though Sasha was still on my mind, Sophie's illness gave me a new perspective, mission and purpose. Even though she was healing, she still wasn't well. I was determined more than ever to get her healthy.

Sasha's lingering absence was the soft white noise in the background of my thoughts, always. I still kept up the search for him, calling his name and walking my neighborhood when I had time, though the searching was becoming less and less frequent. All the while, slowly my hopes were beginning to fade, and a fatalistic type of realization was increasingly becoming a looming reality. A knowing, intuitive part of me was developing a stronger voice for accepting his fate and mine in the situation, but I just didn't want to give up hope or accept that he was gone.

Agnieszka helped so much by being there for Sophie kitten-watch after Debra went home to Phoenix. She covered for me during my work schedule when I would be gone ten to twelve hours at a time, while still working around her own schedule. She learned to give the medications and was vigilant in her devotion to helping Sophie heal. Aga was supportive and nurturing. More importantly, she was there for all the late night phone talks when I was trying to sort it out and simultaneously heal Sophie and grieve for Sasha.

And then suddenly, yet slowly, Sophie started to get better. Between Agnieszka and me, Sophie had the love and regular medicine and support she needed. Her sneezing finally stopped after almost a month of sneezing wetness dispersed constantly and consistently, and she was suddenly breathing better. By mid-September her symptoms were gone. In the end, it took two months for her to be completely well and finally start to feel healthy and happy and free. Her healing happened as most difficult change transpires: seemingly sudden but, in fact, agonizingly slow.

At one point, when she was not getting that much better and I knew the situation could turn either way, I came home late after work and decided to take her outside. I was trying to find a way to give her hope and expectation of a different world for herself other than being miserable and sick. I took her outside to the porch, which faces Glowie, and under a beautiful Carmel night sky while holding her said, "This is yours, you just have to get better. Look at what's waiting for you."

She looked up intently at me, and while still holding my gaze, she began to sniff tentatively the non-eucalyptus fresh air and breathe in the night. She did it repeatedly. She seemed to realize something about her young life. I swear she looked at me as though she had a reckoning. Sophie suddenly looked at me so sweetly and determinedly. She seemed to be in awe of a different world and landscape. At that moment, I knew she was going to make it. I knew she was going to live. And I wondered about my indelible Sasha and if I should begin to let him go. I was constantly, quietly grieving for him but was also hopeful he would be home eventually. I still had no answers for what could have happened to him. It was still so difficult to accept. It was still so sad, but I knew when Sophie filled her lungs with air and didn't sneeze and realized her young life and potential, I was probably not going to see Sasha again. It was a feeling that came over me as strongly as the optimism in my arms in the form of a kitten struggling to heal and a memory that I had been holding onto for over four months since late March.

I chose to start living in the present. So did Sophie. In that moment, under a clear spring Carmel sky and Orion's belt, I started to truly let Sasha go. I don't think I would have had the strength or inclination to move forward if I weren't holding a small miracle of life and survival that needed my attention. Sophie had moved my attention from loss to hope. Even though I tried to deny the feelings, I knew Sophie was giving me the possibility to let Sasha go, on some level, and divert my loss into a new hope and life.

And Then There Was Sophie

Sophie healed and was astonishing in her journey toward living. When Sasha was a kitten, he had Sal to school him, love him and be a companion. Sophie was abandoned the day after she was born and never had a mother's love or suckling or any feline instruction or guidance. Her healing process took several months, and I learned much about her during that time. I learned how strong she was in spirit and unique in personality. I still missed Sasha, but Sophie was a different being, and she eased my heartache with her new ways and personality. She was very different from Sash, but she was remarkable.

Sasha was beautiful, gregarious and completely unique and strong. He had a profound sense of who he was and what he wanted. Sophie was absolutely adorable as a kitten and stunningly beautiful. Her markings are circles and stripes in black and grey. She is athletic yet very feminine. Sasha was athletic, yet clumsy, as though he were always proving his masculine side through sheer will, determination and abandon. But, he was charming beyond belief and seemed to love everyone or at least was willing to give each person an equal chance at earning his praise.

Sophie had been through so much ill health so very young; her focus was solely on me. I think she saw me as her healer, savior, mother. I have no real answer, but she is definitely a one-person cat. She is my cat, and despite her independence and intelligence, she is more aware of me than Sasha had been. Sasha had a huge voice and spirit. Sophie has a small voice but with tremendous range and language. She is much more communicative than Sasha, even though he spoke "human words." Sasha gave everything with abandon, but Sophie is selective will and indiscretion. When she is close, there is no holding back, but she picks her moments, much like me. Sasha never did; he never chose his moments. All of his moments were his, and he lived every day like there was no tomorrow. I sense that Sophie is in for the long run. I hope so, but I still miss my moment guy.

THE QUEEN OF HEARTS

Buried in Snow and Grief

TONY AND TRISH WERE THE ORIGINAL OWNERS of the Sierra Mar Restaurant, and they were bought out of their lease two years after the next-to-worst year of my life and the same year my father died, 2006. When my grandmother died, in December of 2004, the first year of two that brought so much loss and change, I was on a management retreat at Yosemite. The retreat was with Tony and Tricia and the management group of the Sierra Mar Restaurant at the Post Ranch Inn, who were close friends and colleagues.

Our management retreats were legendary in both locale and experience. Paris. Las Vegas. Vancouver twice. Napa. Santa Barbara and more. Tony and Tricia were known within certain circles for their generosity and compassion, mostly within the confines of the family-like atmosphere of the staff at the restaurant. Yet, their generosity was not going unnoticed by the food and beverage industry. It is unusual in the restaurant industry to put a quality of life for employees as a prominent priority, and they did. I certainly came to understand the difference after they were bought out of their lease. My workday went from a conventional eight or nine hours to excessive under the hotel management, which is industry standard. Yet, I believe the food and wine industry doesn't need to be so brutal, heavy and invasive to people who choose to be in service, especially in a high-end situation and experience. Employees are better equipped to deal with the challenges of service when they are rested, working a regular schedule and getting consistent days off. Maybe because I came to this industry through a different background, I always saw the traditional scheduling of doubles and long hours as unproductive and a bit barbaric. I always made sure my employees' needs, desires and considerations were reflected in the schedules I produced. My management style has always been based on supporting and nurturing talent. My feeling was that the industry needed to change, and we did that at Sierra Mar under Tony and Tricia's influence and support. I did it later, after they were gone, with even more independence and drive, but it was always a constant struggle and uphill fight.

They were also known for unorthodox management and good intent. During their tenure, the restaurant was always a mixed bag of irreverent reality infused with passion and elegance. There was no blueprint or formal five-star approach or extreme structure, and it worked for a long time, until there needed to be more. Tricia once told me I was hired because she needed more support to develop the structure the restaurant needed. And we were a good team. Tricia could knock out systems and manuals faster than anyone I have ever known. She was a rock star in that sense. She usually chose Saturday nights to work in the office and develop policy and SOPs. Afterwards, she and Tony would go to the bar for dinner and wine toward the end of dinner service.

It was on one of those Saturdays in early November of '99 that the decision was made to take the management group to France. Tricia, after a few glasses of champagne, pressed Tony to make the trip available to all the staff, not just management, for the lowest rate possible. He smiled and avoided the specifics of her proposal and kept steering the conversation back to the management retreat, about which he was enthusiastic and intrigued. She was relentless and persistent and eventually wore him down. That Saturday night the decision was made and a significant piece of Sierra Mar's history was sealed.

Putting a package together for the staff to consider took at least a hundred hours of research, at a time when there was little Internet research available. Tony relied on Dominique, our wine director, who speaks French, for much of the negotiation and forging. Because of Tony's relentless quest for the best deals possible and his resistance to make a final decision until all resources and options are exhausted, those weeks when they were researching and debating and compromising nearly broke the two of them, both individually and collectively. After pushing Dominique to near manic obsession and exhaustion, they came up with an extremely affordable experience for the staff to travel to the City of Lights. For the Paris trip, Tony and Tricia made the very generous offer to all seventy-plus employees of five days in the city for $600, which included airfare, three meals and hotel accommodations. The package was, again, an unbelievable outpour of generosity. This was who they were and why we all loved working for them. Their decision was well rewarded; Paris and France proved to be a pivotal event for all who made the excursion and a huge growing curve for the restaurant overall.

We had twenty-three staff members in Paris for almost a week, and the food and wine knowledge everyone experienced was life-changing. Yet, what was even more memorable was the camaraderie and closeness we forged as a restaurant and organization from that trip. Everyone would go out for the day with his or her own agenda, and then we would sit in the lounge of our funky, Americana-cinema hotel and share stories. I truly believe we became the world-class restaurant we were eventually known to be because of that trip to Paris. It sparked a passion in everyone who attended the trip to take our restaurant to a higher level. That energy was infectious, and when we got back to California, the seeds were planted.

I have of photo of Eric Paul, Jose, Alix and myself at the Eiffel Tower during that retreat, which now sits near my desk in the front room of the cottage. The temperature was extremely cold on the tower when the photo was taken, yet our looks in the picture display a range of emotions from joy to stoic to foreboding and reflective. Each person in the picture has a different take on the moment. Paris had erected an enormous Ferris wheel near the Eiffel Tower for the millennium that year. It was majestic to see the grandeur of the wheel's presence so close to the tower. There was a moment that passed between us when we recognized we had all finally realized a small dream of standing high above Paris in the tower. The additional awe of looking down on the world's largest Ferris wheel from high above the tower made the moment even more memorable and inspiring.

Yet, every management trip was memorable in its own distinct way and brought the management team closer together. Each trip and event made us better as a respected restaurant, but more importantly, every retreat brought bonding and a deeper understanding of each other. It also brought the chaos and angst most families stumble through under uncertain travel situations. The retreats and trips we took as a management group had a wide range of experience results, but they always made us better as a team as well as a group of individuals who truly cared about one another.

Yosemite was no different. Tony and Tricia rented a sprawling, five-bedroom, two-story, open-beam ranch house in a remote part of the park for the management team and their partners, and we settled in for a bonding excursion and a brief reprieve from our heavy schedules. Nearly all of the retreats were open in respect to partners and spouses accompanying the managers who attended, which gave the retreats a bit of a vacation vibe. The house was so spacious in design and layout that even with twelve of us staying there, most of us never felt cramped or restricted.

The first night we were at the rental house, we had the first cook-off between two teams for dinner and culinary superiority. My team made the meal on the second night. My team spent the first night trying to obtain information about what the competitor was creating even to the extent of secretly videotaping their prep time. It was very competitive and serious, yet hilarious. Because nearly all of the ingredients were brought directly from the vast, unlimited resources of the restaurant's pantry, walk-in and wine cellar, the quality and variety of the dishes presented were over-the-top impressive and decadent. Truffles, foie gras, oysters, chanterelle mushrooms and caviar figured prominently on both team's menus.

During both nights, special wines were paired with each course. Dominique and Tony made it so. Dominique is world-class in his wine knowledge and palate, and Sierra Mar, at that time, had a cellar of at least fifteen thousand wines, so we were definitely spoiled and not without options. Before the dinners, we had champagne with oysters and other appetizers. Our management trip to Alsace, in France, had taught us to appreciate the varietals from that region, specifically Rieslings, Pinot Blancs, Pinot Gris and Gewürztraminers, and they paired beautifully with the rich winter cuisine we were creating for the competition. We also enjoyed some spectacular white Burgundies and a few Italian whites. The red wines focused on Burgundies and Rhones as well as some offbeat Spanish and Italian producers. The first team's dinner was delicious, but I was on Tony's team, and we had a secret weapon for the next night. We had taken a rich veal stock from the restaurant, and we were going to make a French onion soup the next day for our first course. Tony is a life long vegetarian, but he "does stocks."

The second night, during my team's dinner, a monumental snowstorm blew in and covered Yosemite in four feet of snow with drifts even higher. The national park is in the Sierra Nevada mountain range and contains some of the highest elevations in California, with more accumulated snow per year than most of the other ranges in the state. This storm was no exception. It snowed in brilliant white waves of powder and hail. It was like being in the middle of a winter snow globe. It was unrelenting and spectacular. As a child growing up in Pennsylvania, snow was a yearly expectation, like the annual visit of a favorite friend who has moved away but comes back to visit their grandparents. Since I live on the coast now, snow is an event that requires planning, travel and effort. Sadly, I seldom get to the mountains in winter to see my old friend.

The storm blew in overnight, and there was no escape for days. We served our infamous veal stock-infused onion soup course, and it was so successful and well-received that everyone had to take a break from the dinner competition war just to recover from the excess and richness. The dinners were extremely fun and close-knit. The snowstorm on the second night made the sharing and conversation even more special and intimate. The snowstorm created a feeling of isolation while also feeling safe, and I noticed the talk among us was even more relaxed and personal. I went to bed feeling so fortunate and close to the best part of my life.

Alix was with me for the retreat, and even though I had been feeling a major disconnect with her, I was glad she was with me on the trip. She always had a difficult time being "out" with me and had passed on the Sierra Mar Christmas party a week earlier because she was tired and didn't want people to think we were together, though she had gone to most of the retreats we had taken over the years. It was frustrating that this was still an issue so deep into the relationship after fourteen years together.

I woke up the next morning after the storm to find Alix looking at me with love and sadness and intent. It was the same look she had when she told me Seth had been in a horrific accident the first week of September 2001. When I woke up in Yosemite, she had the same tender love and support. Not wanting me to hear the news over the phone, my mom had called early in the morning and told her. Alix knew her partner, and she broke the news of my grandmother's death swiftly and with love. It had been too soon after Eric Paul. It had been eight months. Eric Paul died in April, and my grandmother went to bed on December 7th and never woke up. She had not been ill, and while Eric Paul's death had been devastating, losing my grandmother unexpectedly was the loss I couldn't handle. My grandmother was my anchor all of my life. I cried from the deepest place while being buried in snow without an escape. My close friends and co-workers gave me the support and the distance I needed. I am forever in their debt for how lovingly they responded to my grief. Their love had so much simultaneous warmth and lightness; their humor eventually gave me solace.

The first day of knowing about my grandmother's death I tried to be strong and not bring the energy down from the fun we were having at the retreat, but I was absolutely raw and hurting. I had just begun to get some semblance of balance back from losing Eric Paul. Alix and I had taken a real adult vacation in November and had gone to Moorea in the South Pacific. We stayed in a hut over the ocean with our own dock for snorkeling and a glass floor in the living room where we could see fish anytime we wanted.

As magical as it was, I knew my fourteen-year relationship with Alix was ending, even though that thought absolutely terrified me. I remember being on the island and struggling with the overwhelming feeling that I couldn't hide anymore, especially in my relationship. I once read that tragedy and loss will make a person look at all aspects of their life with a clear eye and different perspective. After Eric died, I saw my life with a new lens and different feelings. I felt like I was falling in slow motion down a dark corridor, and now my grand-mother was gone as well. That first day of knowing she was gone seemed to accelerate the feeling of falling into something I couldn't see. Even though I was surrounded by affection, I felt alone and isolated by the sudden loss. I remember thinking, "How much can a person handle?" I eventually understood. It depends on the person. It depends on the circumstances.

The second day after I learned about my grandmother's passing, Tony and Dominique enticed me into making an igloo out of all of the snow on the deck. It was a monumental task since the snow was higher than the door. Alix had been nurturing and caring the first day, as always, and once she got me interested in tunneling and building in the snow, I knew it would be therapeutic and even fun in a "I feel fun in a numb kind of way." They made a treasure hunt out of building the igloo with prizes inserted into various parts of the tunnel and fort. Tony made weird nude snow sculptures and made me laugh. An impossible task on the day I had feared my entire life. My grandmother was a true force of love in my life, and the day I had dreaded forever had finally come. She was gone. And I was thousands of miles away from her.

An Impossible Funeral

All my life my grandmother would say to me at the strangest times, "I don't want you to come to my funeral. I don't want you to see me that way." It was an unusual mantra, and I used to just smile and say back to her, "Of course I will be at your funeral."

And then she would say, "I don't want you there."

It was such an unusual discourse because we were so close, and she said it so many times throughout my life. She said it so many times over the years I would get annoyed by the words as I grew older. I never understood why she kept bringing it up with me.

She got her wish in the end. There was no way for me to tunnel out from the storm in time to travel the three thousand miles to where she was being laid to rest. I would not make it to her funeral. I couldn't have gotten there, no matter how much I tried. Yet, I was fortunate to be surrounded by friends and love through such a heart-break and loss, and even though I tried to hold my gut-wrenching grief in check, I felt safe to feel what was necessary and what I couldn't hold back. I have come to understand our angels are always watching over us and give us what we need.

While I was buried in snow in Yosemite, I wrote a eulogy for my grandmother, which my mother read for me at the service. I wrote it while we were painting portraits of each other in our large rental house with the fire blazing and everyone cozy during the retreat. It was after the fort and igloo building and a long walk I took with Alix and Tricia.

We had drawn names and were given the task to draw the person whose name we drew. It was part of a team building exercise Tony had devised, but it was laid-back, intimate and fun. Tony was always creating competitions and, even though some of them are not laid-back, they are always interesting and often hilarious. On previous management retreats we had biked competitively through a park in Vancouver in December rain and sleet, stopped for a quick game of miniature bowling in a strange dive bar while on our way to an expensive dinner, and on the same trip he rented a curling rink for several hours so we could discover the competetive joys of one of the strangest events of the winter Olympics. (It was, surprisingly, quite fun.)

The portrait drawing competition turned out to be poignant and a life memory. The closeness we all shared from the drawing exercise was remarkable. While everyone was sketching, there was a stillness intermixed with soft laughter and tenderness. Trish drew my name and sketched while I was writing the eulogy. She captured me perfectly. She captured the moment. I still have the portrait in my bedroom. When I look at her intimate drawing of me, I don't see sadness anymore. I just see strength. Even in such a dark moment in my life, she saw who I was before I knew.

EULOGY FROM YOSEMITE

Gin

❝MY GRANDMOTHER WAS ONE OF THE HEROES OF MY LIFE. I had the great privilege of being her first grandchild, born to her first child, and my place in her world was secured forever. She was my "Gin." The story goes that I couldn't say "Grandma," and I called her "Gin," which, much to her chagrin, stuck and then she was everyone else's Gin as well.

Some of the sweetest parts of my childhood are laced with her presence and influence. Staying at my grandparents' dairy farm as a child in the sixties and seventies was an adventure any child would have treasured, but my grandmother provided the secret charms that made it truly magical. From a child's perspective, the house my grandmother ran seemed to hold candy and treats in every corner of every space. From the cavernous wall-size meat locker in the basement, which held every ice cream treat known to Western Pennsylvania at that time, to the candy bin in the white cabinet next to the stove, a child was never wanting for sweet treasures in her house. The palatial meat locker was for storing the red meat from the butchered animals, but she used it for treats, which seemed to have more influence than the directive of the farm's protocol. I loved when she would take me to that huge freezer and let me choose my treat for the day. It was seductive and alluring. I was a slightly chubby kid back then, and ice cream was my nirvana. She never made me feel bad for the indulgence. She actually encouraged it.

She was famous for her homemade donuts and fried chicken, which she made every Labor Day weekend for the annual picnic at the fair. My uncle would show cows during the fair. My grandfather's farm, Beulah Farms, was named for the road beyond the white fencing and pastures. Beulah Farms was always a serious competitor at every county and regional fair. Gin was protective of her donuts, though, and always held back donut holes for my brother, sister and me. Walking into the house at the farm when she was making donuts was intoxicating and euphoric for a child. They were delicious, and we gobbled them up as fast as she could put them on our plates.

I always had the sense that the farmhouse was her domain. My grandfather had the farm to run, and my grandmother had the house, as well as her chores in the barn, to take care of, but the house was her refuge, her sanctuary. My introduction to jazz and big band was through Gin. She loved the music of the forties, and those tunes played softly on the radio from any room in which she was working. She was always working. I don't remember her ever really sitting still until she got older. I loved listening to those radios with her, watching her work, listening to her banter. She was strong and could be tough, but she was tender and funny and could love a young child sweetly. She loved to spoil and to give, and her generosity was a great part of who she was. She gave freely without motives or attachments, and I never remember leaving a visit without a new outfit or shoes or five dollars to buy something new with, which was a small fortune in those days.

This is what I remember about my grandmother, about Gin. She gave love unconditionally, like grandmothers do, but with a devotion a grandchild could build part of their life on. Most children have a gawky stage during childhood, but mine seemed to last the better part of a decade. Gin always told me how beautiful I would be, and she was so convinced of it that I eventually converted to believing it as well. I believe my ability to have an eternal belief in positive outcomes, and a truly grounded belief in who I am, came from those early years and the mantra of her words. She would tell me repeatedly how tremendous and wonderful I was. She always believed and was so convincing it made me believe forever.

She could be outspoken in her opinions, but she always sympathized with those who required it most. Likewise, she was most tender with those she most felt sympathy for and needed someone to give voice to their situations. She could do this with great pursuit, and sometimes it was exhausting. She was kind and giving of her time and resources, and she could work longer and harder than anyone I know. She was a child of the Great Depression, but she was determined not to let anyone she loved go without.

I was blessed to be with her most of the last week of her life. She was diminished, but not defeated. She was courageous and seemingly focused on a long recovery. We played cards, something I have done with her since childhood. She taught me nearly all the card games I know, and I never beat her until I was well into adulthood.

Even on my last visit, she was correcting my scorekeeping, a position of honor and authority she only recently relinquished. Even though I am surrounded by a wonderful family and loving friends, I can't imagine my life without her. I can't imagine not talking to her on the phone every week or hearing her messages. She gave me strength and security and an unrelenting love. She made me laugh, always. She had a hundred sayings, which were hers alone, and now I will have to remember them from the distant echoes of the past. She was my grandmother, but she was one of my best friends. To say my life was enriched because of her is a vast understatement. Her passing leaves a void for all of us that can never be filled. But, I will remember her as one of the great heroes of my life."

In Retrospect

My mother is an excellent public speaker. She delivered the eulogy with her deft touch and timing for comedy. I look now at what I wrote in the fortress of Yosemite and realize how short it fell and how far my words have come. I could have done so much better by the one who mattered so much.

Waiting for Me

I'd gone back to Pennsylvania to see Gin that November of 2004, after Thanksgiving of that same year when Eric Paul died and a few weeks after Alix and I vacationed in Moorea. The same year when everything just seemed to unravel and move painfully forward at the same time. We had a wonderful visit in so many ways. My grandmother had been living with my Aunt Jane and Uncle Tom for several years. They have a home next to the farm my grandfather and grandmother owned for most of my childhood where my mother grew up. My memories of the farm are some of the best of my childhood. It is where I learned about hard work, how animals are butchered, where milk comes from and how the world, my world, functioned. Being back in Pennsylvania and next to the farm is always bittersweet for me. There are so many memories. I tend to feel things too deeply and being there is like opening a floodgate. My family is intense. It is how I was raised, and it doesn't give me concern anymore, except when it does.

Yet, that November visit was mystical and sweet and I knew on some level it was also an ending. Even though I couldn't consider that possibility then. I can never consider endings until they are forced upon me. We watched Lifetime Christmas movies every night and talked about the past while looking at its images in photographs. Photos of my mother and her siblings. Photos of me as a baby. Photos of my siblings at every age. My grandmother's few baby pictures. Photos of the farm throughout the decades from black and white to color, from a simple operation to a state-of-the-art business the years before my grandfather sold. Photographs of the elders from generations before, stern and sad and somehow knowing. So many of the photos I had seen before, but they still felt fresh in their recognition. It was familiar and lovely. Families almost always want you closer than you are able to accommodate, and I really felt during this stay how much they wanted to be in my life. I was close during the visit, but I always keep a separation wall in my life and quietly use it to my advantage.

I took a walk in the hills around the farm my grandparents used to own the second day I was there. It was the opening day of deer season, which is quite a big event in Pennsylvania. My aunt made sure I had bright colors on to ensure safety. Even with bright colors, I still encountered semi-coherent hunters asking me for directions.

"Hey you. Hello. I like your jacket. Have you seen any deer? Bucks?"

"No, I haven't."

"Nice jacket. I'm sorry if I scared you. Have you seen any deer?"

"No, I haven't. "

"Are you lost?"

"No, I'm good."

"Let me know if you see anything. Are you hunting?"

"No, just taking a walk."

"Look out for the deer, ok?"

I was so relieved the deer were smarter than their pursuers. I hiked back to the house and felt like I had escaped a bullet myself. Aunt Jane was relieved I was in one piece. We celebrated with Klondike ice cream bars, and I helped her decorate their artificial Christmas tree while, once again, we watched a Lifetime Christmas movie.

The hills around the farm are childhood beautiful to me. As a child, I dreamed about my future and my life while gazing at them. I loved how we could see other towns in the distance from our vista at the farm. The hills and mountains and trees of my childhood made me feel safe, when sometimes my world did not. This was coal and steel country. Even though the Appalachians are not as momentous as I remember as a child, they stir awe in me still. The people living there are from a variety of ethnic backgrounds, with Italian, Polish and Slavic being prominent. I grew up with friends who had amazingly difficult-to-pronounce last names, but it didn't seem unusual to me. It was just life in a small community with colorful people and complicated subplots, when you knew their back-stories but not always the story itself.

I left when I was sixteen, against my will, because my father took a job in Illinois, even though we moved to Indiana. The schools were supposedly better in the Hoosier State and my father's commute was only thirty minutes from the very small town we "embraced." I think we moved to Indiana because the people in the very, very small town we moved to were safe and the property values were encouraging. The move to Indiana was extremely difficult for our family, especially for Mark and my sister and me. Seth was only six so he adapted more quickly and with less drama than the rest of us. There were no Italian, Polish or Slavic names in Indiana, and the blandness was sometimes torturous.

My stay with my grandmother and aunt was for five days during that visit in '04, and I embraced every moment because something beyond me knew it was important. The bedroom I slept in was a room with a bed, yet also housed all of the extras the house needed to hold. I love my aunt and uncle, but they are collectors of every thing imaginable. I was surrounded with memorabilia: a Life Strider, baskets full of clothes, rugs and random household objects, a ceramic deer on a clock, pictures in envelopes, pictures in frames, moments in time captured throughout the room, my aunt's various workout gear, two vacuum cleaners of various sizes and functions, small treasures from trips and moments. One of my favorite photos in the room was a picture of my aunt and great-grandfather taken at the county fair in the early sixties. They are both immersed in reading the local paper. There is nothing specific about the photo, but throughout my childhood, I used to stare at it and feel a connection. It is in black and white and subtly captures the era.

When I would go to sleep in my guest room, I felt like the room was alive and I was about to be swallowed whole. Many of the items in the bedroom seemed to have their own energy, and being sensitive, the room felt noisy even in the dark. Sleep was often my nemesis then, and I tried hard not to feel as though I were falling asleep in the middle of a rummage sale. It was a great visit though. My grandmother was amazingly lucid and loving, as always. She told me the family stories I cherish and now need to hold sacred because they are part of the family lore. My family doesn't really talk about the past. For me, my grandmother was the connecting thread to all of the family mysteries and outcomes, even though that thread was distinctly her perspective or opinion. Often, I longed for more information and a deeper understanding. Family history, myths and lore have many voices and points of view. Still, her presence and love was engaging and encompassing. Throughout the entire visit, I focused on holding on to the sound of her voice. I wanted those notes to stay inside me, echoing softly and reverberating when I needed them most.

My aunt and uncle were gracious hosts, and I reconnected with them quickly after not seeing them for so many years. Even though our worlds are worlds apart, the difference in lifestyles and priorities faded away after a few days. They are homespun and grounded in their singular way of looking at their world. They are plain spoken yet deeply immersed in their linear approach to their routines and beliefs, which structure their lives. We played cards, ate dinner at five o'clock, watched the ever-present Lifetime network Christmas movies and shared stories and space in the casual, relaxed, nonchalant way that is usually reserved for family. We played canasta, gin rummy and 500 rummy with enthusiasm, pursuit and intent. I love my aunt because of her loving nature and nondescript approach to life. She is as gracious in explaining a new card game as she is in giving comfort and support. During this visit, I realized I had missed knowing her and who she had been all these years while I was away.

As for card playing, my grandmother had loved playing cards her whole life, and nothing got past her. Her favorite games were 500 rummy, gin rummy, hearts, Uno, solitaire, and crazy eights, but her absolute card playing passion focused solely on canasta. She could play for hours and hours at a time, and I never saw her turn down a request for another game until the last year of her life when she would tire more quickly. Playing cards with her was a comfort of idle talk, secrets shared, fantastic stories, strongly noted opinions but, most of all, unbridled laughter. Until it came to keeping score.

"Did you count that score? Did you get my hand?"

"Yes, I counted it," I would respond with a smile.

"Yes, but did you see I had two hundred points here?" she would continue.

"I counted all of your canastas."

"I know, but you missed my wild cards."

"No, I got them."

"Are you sure, Wandie?"

"Yes, I am sure," I said again with a smile.

I told Eric Paul about "Wandie" once, and he pounced on using it. I told him only one person in the world got to call me that name. He still used it, but he chose his moments carefully. He used it so seldom, and only in the moments that seemed very special, that I forgave him for taking the sacred rights of my grandmother to a new level.

I called her "Lucky Dog" because she was and had earned it

through countless trumpings she had given me in card games over the years. And, for all of the indelible hard times and trumpings she had taken and overcome throughout her life. For many reasons, I just liked calling her that. She was my "lucky dog."

During that visit, my Gin talked to me every evening late into the night, when my aunt and uncle had gone to bed. She always did. When I was young, she would lie with me until I fell asleep, and her talk was mesmerizing. Yet, she would wear me out with her ongoing concerns, insights and musings. I used to worry about her because she never seemed to sleep. I literally never saw her sleep until I was in my thirties, and even then she would deny it, saying, "I wasn't asleep. I just had my eyes shut."

During those late night talks when I was young, she talked to me as a confidant and an adult with guarded territories. I remember her trust made me feel special, but her stories and distress, especially about my mom and dad, made me realize, even more, what I long suspected even as a child. The world can be a complicated, hurtful mess. Ever an optimist, though, I took pride in putting a positive spin on her fears and doubts. When I stayed with her as a child, I would often fall asleep to "I hope you are right, Wandie. I hope you are right."

Staying up with her that last visit felt so close and familiar; the closeness and love meant everything to me, and I hope she knew as well. She would hold my hand and tell me stories about her life, many I knew by heart and memory, and some that I didn't. She would tire easily, though, which was new territory, but she held my hand till she fell asleep, and I would stay and watch for as long as needed or desired. After so many years of working long hours, of working through the night to get her housework done after working in the barn all day, after so many years of lost sleep, now, when she finally fell asleep first, I noticed how peacefully she slept. She was in her early eighties during that visit yet, in her sleep, she seemed ageless. I could see her youthful, childhood self on her sleeping, soft face. I willed myself to remember every part of her, every part of those moments. After a while I would slip away to my overstocked rummage sale room and try to sleep.

I remember my last image of her. I had to be at the Pittsburg airport by ten o'clock in the morning. My uncle was driving me, and it was a two-hour car ride, which meant we left six hours before my flight because that is his time management and how seriously he takes his responsibilities and worries.

When we drove away in the wee hours of the morning, and I am not a wee hour in the morning kind of person in any way, I looked back at the yellow brick house in the darkness and saw my aunt and my grandmother looking intently yet sweetly out of the kitchen window. My grandmother seemed even smaller framed in the window, and she seemed as innocent and trusting as a young child. They were waving good-bye. A small kitchen light was shining above them, which created a stark but revealing illumination. They looked so sincere and intent on their message. I will never forget the way Gin was waving. It was innocent and childlike and from the heart. Her enthusiastic waving was so loving it was heartbreaking. I remember feeling that moment and knowing it was special and important and forever. A small voice said, "What if that is your last moment? What if you never see her again?"

Another voice said, "She loves me so much. It is so very difficult to leave her. I love her beyond and even in the blackness of morning, she is still light. She will be with you for a long time. "

Both voices were true.

SHINY OBJECTS AND STRINGS FOR THE AGES

Letting Her Go

I N HER FIRST NINE MONTHS, I had learned to keep Sophie close and had trained her on a leash about "outside time." I didn't want to lose another cat to infinite, unknown outcomes, and whenever she was outside, I was with her or she was on a harness. She was getting frustrated with the process, and I was feeling like I was trying to control outcomes that were not rooted in reality. They were based on loss and the unknown and my own fear. They were based on the past. One warm, sunny day, she was on the leash in the backyard under the huge oak tree while I was gardening, and I decided, in that moment, to let her live her life, whatever that would be. I was tired of being cautious and afraid. I unclipped the leash, and she looked at me with wonder and then alternated staring at the sky and the new-found vastness of the backyard for several minutes. Eventually, she looked at me with the appearance of a huge smile and then ran laps around the house. Someone else used to do that.

Yet, this was her moment, and it was heartwarming to see her so happy. The release and relief she displayed on her face and entire being was so visible and deep-felt it was palpable. There was no going back to the leash or controlling her movements. Every living being needs to be free within the confines of their life, and Sophie was no different and neither was I. By unleashing her, I let go of some of myself in the process. I was holding on too closely to much of my life, and Sophie was a part of that control. I was worried something bad would happen to her if I let her go. I was worried something bad would happen to me if I let her explore her world. I needed to trust the universe again and myself. When Sophie got her freedom, I felt something heavy release in me. As she was looking at the sky and then running laps around the house, I felt the best and most hopeful I had felt in a long time. I felt free.

The Next Summer - 2009

Debra was due in for her yearly visit, and that always mixes the most important elements of the family chemistry chart with combustion and torque. In other words, one of my favorite times of the year was about to happen, my yearly, exclusive visit with my sister. It was a few days before her arrival, and I was lying on the couch reading *New Yorker* on a precious day off. Sophie had jumped the wall in the yard and was gone for more than her usual few hours. She was now a rambunctious one-year-old feline, and even though she only goes outside in the daytime, she has been known to take off for brief neighborhood sojourns, especially on my days off when I let her outside longer than her normal schedule. I can't explain the feeling that came over me while I was reading, but it seemed to be guided by something or someone outside my realm. I was a little worried about Sophie being gone, and she was in the back of my mind, but Sasha was suddenly a familiar white noise surrounding me in a way that was requiring my attention and notice.

In the fifteen months since his disappearance, Sasha was never far from my thoughts or heart, and I often could still feel his energy in the cottage and yard. For months and months, even after I brought kitten Sophie home from the SPCA, I was hopeful that Sasha would return or be found. For as long as I could, I held on to the hope that he would come home. Much like I held on to the belief in Santa Clause when I was a child because I didn't want to cause doubt for my younger siblings. Then, about three months after Sash was missing, my neighbor Jean, from across the street, stopped me on my way to work one day and asked about Sasha. She, like most of the people on my street, knew him from his gregarious outings and was fond of him.

Jean had been the mayor of Carmel after Clint Eastwood's term in the early nineties. She was the first neighbor I met when I moved in, and I immediately liked her no-nonsense approach and warmth she applied to monitoring the neighborhood. As time went on, we eventually became two of the only full-time residents on our street, and we kept an eye out for each other. One spring, when she was getting ready to leave for her annual road trip to observe the wildflowers in the desert, she came over and told me she was leaving for three weeks. She wanted me to know because she knew I worked late hours and was worried about not being home in case there was any trouble. Over the years, I appreciated her concern, kindness and toughness.

"Any word on Sasha?" she asked that day.

"No, nothing. I'm trying to stay hopeful, but it has been several months now."

A strange look came over her face, serious though passionate. It seemed she was trying to make a decision about the direction of our conversation. She hesitated for a noticeable moment and then said, "Did Lucinda tell you about the blood on her driveway? They found it right around the time Sasha disappeared."

Lucinda was my next-door neighbor. We had forged a friendship when she and her husband, Derrick, had popped their heads over the fence that afternoon a few years ago when I had first moved in and was attempting to clear the excessive growth and ivy in the backyard. Back when I thought I could conquer nature's will by myself. Sasha loved lying on their driveway. Lucinda and Derrick were also two of my many neighbors who had a second home in Carmel. They were usually only in town one week a month, so I had not seen them very often since Sasha went missing.

Jean's words about the blood felt like a punch to the stomach. I must have had a stunned and hurt look on my face because she immediately said, "I wanted to tell you earlier, but didn't want you to worry even more. I just thought you should have that information."

She said it so sincerely yet so directly, like a doctor yanking off a blood-soaked Band-Aid in one swift motion. "No, thank you for telling me," I stammered as I looked down at the ground to get my bearings. "It's difficult to hear, but I need to know. Thank you."

I got into the car and began to drive to Big Sur to my busy schedule for the day, but not before I pulled over after I was out of sight of Jean and cried the grief of having to contemplate the ending for Sasha I had been dreading and unwilling to fully acknowledge or accept. It was a difficult day and one I had feared since Sash vanished in March.

It took me several months to approach Lucinda about the blood. As mentioned, they are only in town every four to six weeks, and I didn't want to bother her or be intrusive. I also didn't want to know the truth. When I finally got up the nerve to talk to her in late summer, two months after Jean spoke with me, she was gardening in her exquisite yard. She was wearing gardening clogs and gloves. With her hair pulled back into a tight bun and her t-shirt and jeans, she glowed with an ageless air of enthusiastic optimism mixed with wisdom.

"Hi, Lucinda. Can I talk to you for a moment?"

"Of course. What's up?"

"Jean mentioned to me a while ago that there was blood on your driveway around the time that Sasha disappeared."

She stopped working and stood up to look directly at me. She gave me such a soft look of compassion; her look was tender yet heartbreaking. Still, she didn't hesitate in talking to me in straight terms, and I was grateful for her honesty.

"There was blood. We found it a few days later when we got in."

"Was there a lot of blood?" I practically whispered.

She looked me square in the eye and held my gaze for a few moments and then said quietly, "There was a lot of blood."

There was a long moment of silence between us, and then she said with her calm confidence, "That doesn't mean it was Sasha. Don't give up faith that he might be coming home."

We stood in awkward silence for an uneasy ten or fifteen seconds, which felt like minutes, and then I thanked her for being honest and talking to me. But we both knew the outcome and the truth. In that exact moment, I knew Sasha was never going to be with me again.

All of these thoughts were swirling around my subconciousness that late June day when I was trying to relax on my day off but was worried about Sophie being gone for a few hours. I still found myself projecting my own fear about unknown outcomes with felines when she was gone too long. In fact, letting her outside had been a difficult decision, but I could see the joy she had in enjoying her wonderful Carmel yard and home base. I could see the difference in her confidence by letting her explore her world. I knew I had to get over my own fears about loss in letting her have a controlled and monitored outdoor life. All of her delayed time away invoked a muscle memory of loss about Sasha and other absences from my life. I knew I needed to let go of the anxiety of suspecting loss when souls I loved were temporarily missing. Still, sometimes it is difficult to know the difference.

On that day in June, when Sasha's history of love and loss was suddenly so pronounced, I found myself calmly and distinctly putting down my *New Yorker* and walking outside. I did not hesitate or deliberate. Something within and beyond my consciousness seemed to be dictating. It was as though I were listening to a higher power or voice. I walked directly to the backyard of Glowie, the house next door that was built in the early nineteen hundreds and recently sold, its fate sealed for destruction for a modern Carmel uplift.

I went to the backyard and stared at the backside of Glowie. There was quite a bit of debris, tree limbs and weed growth. It felt sad and a bit creepy, as though the state of disrepair had fallen to an even lower state of sadness and neglect. As I stood in the backyard, I noticed a small door with a latch in the back of the house, which seemed to lead to a crawlspace. I don't know why I had never gone to this door when we were looking for Sasha. I had gone to this house repeatedly during his absence and called his name. This house was thirty feet from my porch, and I had called his name for over a year, especially on the sad, dark nights when I was missing him so very much. Why had I never paid more attention to the latch on this door? I had initially dismissed it because it was locked, but then I realized, standing there in front of it that June day, there were concrete blocks missing on the back right side foundation of Glowie. An animal could get into that same space, which was possibly connected to the latched door. I had looked into the space where the concrete blocks were missing many, many times and saw nothing. Perhaps the area where the blocks were missing had access to the area behind the door I had dismissed for over a year.

In an instant, my heart sank and my mind did the calculations. It seemed like I stood staring at the door for a long time. Time seemed to escape me, and after a long while, I approached it slowly. My heart was racing a bit, and I took a deep breath. I gathered courage and opened the latch and door slowly.

When I was staring at the latched door, I wondered again why I had never opened it when I had been looking for him for so long. This was one of his favorite hang-outs of all his neighborhood places, and I had looked here again and again when he was missing. When I had Agnieszka's 29th birthday party at my house the year before, he went outside because of all of the fuss and noise that the party was generating. Yet, as soon as the last guest left, he jumped over the fence from Glowie and walked in nonchalant and loving, ready to be close with me and go to sleep. It was as though he always knew what was going on with me and what we both needed out of a situation. When he jumped over the fence after the last guest left, I was so relieved to see him because I was worried about him, and we always had a sense of each other. I realized the night of Agnieszka's party we were now simpatico to a level of unprecedented trust and affection.

I opened the hatch to the underbelly of Glowie. After adjusting my eyes to the late afternoon light, I could see a skeleton with a few orange hairs lying far and deep into the crawl space. I had extreme trepidation about crawling to the bones within my sight. I stared at them for a long time before I began my descent into the darkness. I kept willing my eyes to see something different. I am best with death with my eyes half closed or with my glasses removed. I did neither as I began my crawl through the cobwebs, but the approaching darkness created a dim filter. The approach was creepy, difficult and lonely. After all of my hesitation in psyching myself to do this, the sun had gone lower in the sky making the visibility more difficult. I crawled as long as I could bear and then stared intently at the bones in the very back of the crawlspace. The crawl space was about forty feet deep, and I crawled within eight feet of the skeleton. I looked as hard as I could. I pushed down my uneasiness about the small space and dread and fear of finding him. I stared as long as I could withstand and then backed out uneasily and shut the door. I walked quickly back to the cottage, shaking off what I had just done and what I had just seen and tried to slow down my mind and emotions. I couldn't deal with the evidence. I couldn't deal with the thought of the evidence. In the matter of a few moments, my entire reality shifted, even though it was playing out like a dream sequence, and I was reluctant to wake up and process the material. Sophie came back shortly, and I went about my night, but the skeleton under Glowie never left my thoughts. And I knew, but I didn't want to know.

As darkness started to overtake the June day, after trying to read and relax but doing neither, I decided to go back to Glowie with a flashlight and look again. The skeleton was more real in the near darkness with my light. I stared and disparaged myself for not crawling in all the way to look more thoroughly. I just couldn't bring myself to go completely to what I thought was him. I was filled with so much sadness and remorse and denial. But I knew. And in my silence I tried to prepare for the inevitable. All night long, I thought about what I believed I had seen but wasn't certain I had witnessed. Yet, I couldn't bring myself to confirm what I knew in my heart.

Theater Talk

The next day I met Agnieszka for a late afternoon movie. I was feeling distant from her. I was feeling distance from my own space in my life in general. We were sitting through the commercials and the long intro to get to the previews, which I find annoying and time killing. We were quiet and then I decided to tell her about the orange-tufted skeleton under Glowie. The distance between us evaporated, and she listened intently as her demeanor softened with empathy and concern. After the movie was over, she said quietly, "I want to come to your house and look at the crawl space."

I was feeling defensive and afraid and not wanting help, but knew I needed it. She followed me to the cottage in her car, and then we took a flashlight and went to the now ominous door. Agnieszka stared at the latch with a slightly worried look on her face and hesitated for a moment. She seemed to draw a steady, deep breath and then said quietly, "Ok." And with that said, she unlocked the door to Glowie's basement and stared into the greyness. Even though it was still daylight, it was difficult to see under the house. She crawled into the space until she was a few feet from the skeleton and stared for a long while. When she turned to look at me, she had a look of stoic sadness.

"Do you think it is Sasha?" I asked.

She gave me eyes of love but said nothing. Then quietly said, "I'm not sure."

We both knew what was true. To this day, I love her for not saying more.

Savior

Soon afterward, I called Lori Trew, my office manager and close friend. Throughout the difficult period when Sash was missing a year before, she was instrumental in grounding me through the loss of his disappearance and giving immeasurable support in trying to understand his vanishing from my life. She loves cats and has a deep knowledge of their behaviors and moods. Her husband is a renaissance man, and one of his hobbies is taxidermy. He does carpentry, maintenance, electrical, painting, builds furniture and more. He is also a cat lover and fearless in most everything. When I told Lori about the skeletal discovery with a few tufts of orange fur, she went into her effective problem-solving modus operandi immediately. Her organization skills and ability to get things done efficiently were renowned and respected at the restaurant. It was also who she was as a person, and I was grateful for her take-charge attitude about Glowie's crawlspace, even though I was worried about the outcome.

"This is what we are going to do. I'm sending Greg to your house the day after tomorrow. I know you are taking a few days off for Debra's visit, but Greg will be in town to do some errands and he can look at the crawlspace." When I hesitated and looked away to contemplate how quickly this was happening, she put her hands squarely on my shoulders and said firmly but gently, "Don't worry.

He'll take care of everything."

Greg and Lori live on the south coast of Big Sur and they don't come to town very often. I sensed she was sending him in to take care of what I couldn't bring myself to do.

"Are you sure?" I asked. "This could be a bit gruesome."

"He loves this stuff. A few months ago he found a bird skeleton and brought it home to put back together. It was disgusting but beautiful. Please let him help you."

And so I did the thing for which I am not naturally disposed. I let him help me. I needed to know if Sasha were lying under Glowie, and I couldn't do it on my own.

The Things My Sister Brings

Debra flew in the next day. It was great to see her and reconnect. Deb and I settled in, like we do every year, with great conversation and the slow process toward getting caught up on our lives and getting to know each other again. That process is always magical to me because it comes in waves and movements and has its own timeline. Wine, later in the night, always makes the seams fall away and the laughter more accessible. Even though it is not necessary, it speeds up the reconnection and solidifies the memories and the absurdity of life and our shared life in general.

On her first day, we drove to Pacific Grove to her favorite yarn store, and she fell into the stupor she reserves for instant, yet long-deprived, gratification. My sister is a teacher of many things and a master of more. She is hip and cool, even though she doesn't think so anymore. I love watching her exuberant contentment at the yarn store. She still gets excited about the textures of wool and cotton in their many forms. It takes me back to when we lived together and she used "knitting therapy" to heal from her divorce. We had a great first day together. We made dinner and watched Tales of Despereaux.

Eventually, I talked to Deb about Sasha.

She was extremely supportive while astonished and unnerved that he could be found a year later and still identified. We talked through many scenarios about his final day and the year that had passed with him decomposing so close to my home. After some wine, we had convinced ourselves that maybe it wasn't him, but that scenario didn't last very long. She was tired and fell asleep early. I stayed up a bit longer and went outside to look at Glowie and think about Sasha lying underneath the house. I thought about the psychic's prediction about Sasha being in a crawlspace. I struggled with equal measures of guilt, anger and sadness though they ebbed and flowed at conflicting levels. I wanted to go over with a flashlight again and see him but couldn't muster the nerve. I knew Greg would be coming tomorrow, and the mystery would be over soon enough. I knew reality would find me in tomorrow's light. I tried to enjoy the darkness for a few more hours. What if it weren't Sasha? What if? And fell asleep in those promises and lures.

Savior Extraordinaire

Greg arrived the next day, as promised, but with a vigorous, Navy Seal, ready manner. I actually wasn't ready for such a zealous approach because I was still processing the possibility of Sasha's skeleton being found so close to my house. I was still trying to understand: If that were him, how did I not know he was there, so close yet beyond reach? I was trying to find a way to handle the sadness and closure I was feeling without its affecting Debra's visit and our time together.

Greg came to my house with supportive enthusiasm. He seemed excited in his undertaking. He brought a shovel, tarp and blanket, as well as flashlights and an army surplus bag full of items that could not be seen. I walked him over to Glowie and opened the latched door and showed him the skeleton image at the end of the crawlspace.

On the far right of the house, Greg noticed other openings to the crawlspace from missing cinder blocks in the foundation.

"It looks like animals could gain access to the crawlspace over there in those openings."

"Yeah, I didn't think that area connected to the crawlspace. I looked in that area where the openings are many, many times," I said softly.

Sasha always hung out in the area where the cinder blocks were missing. Why had I not searched there when it mattered so? The thought kept playing a loop in my mind that I couldn't stop.

Greg did not hesitate for an instant but crawled rather quickly to where the skeleton was lying so perfectly intact and did an analysis. He did what I could not do. He crawled the entire forty feet or so of the crawlspace and was practically on top of the skeleton of bones and orange fur. I looked at the sky and the ground and waited uncomfortably. I was numb with anticipation and fear. After several minutes, he came out from under the house and announced with sad conviction that the skeleton was definitely a cat with a few tufts of orange fur left. He said quietly, "I think it is Sasha. What do you want me to do? Should I bring him out?"

"Yes. Are you okay with that?"

I was not sure what the right words were to answer him. I was filled with dread but also curiosity. He was eager and confident in his response, and it gave me comfort.

"I've done a lot of taxidermy and will bring him out in one piece. It will be okay. I promise."

His quiet, soft assurances made my heart finally accept what was happening. Sasha was dead. I knew where he died. His remains were about to be very real to me. He was never coming home, yet he was in a way. And I was so very grateful for that simple, awful truth...and gift.

I went back to the house and left Greg to do what he does best. I had known him for a few years, and I knew he would make it right. He always does. Still, there were too many emotions running through my body. I kept walking through my house trying to do something constructive, but I couldn't focus on any single task. I called Agnieszka, and she said she would come over, but I told her to take her time and come by later on her way to work.

After an hour or so, Greg came to the front door and told me he had Sasha intact and safely in a box. I was touched that he brought a special box for the extrication. He asked if I wanted to see him. I told him I wasn't ready. I knew I would probably never be able to see him in skeleton form. I never had gotten used to looking at the many dead objects Sasha brought home or left for me. And this was Sasha. This was my Sasha.

"He is perfect in his structure. He bled out, I believe, because there are no visible signs of any wounds that he was mangled or struggled. I really think he died peacefully."

I looked at the box. I could tell Greg was eager for me to look at Sasha, though he had him covered with a towel. His words were comforting, yet strange, because I was reeling and trying not to be sick. Yet, the entire time after Greg brought his body out from Glowie he was coaching me through the process of understanding what was happening and what his thoughts were on Sasha's final hours. I had spent so much time thinking about Sasha's last hours that I should have been ready to hear a taxidermist's expert opinion about what those hours were, but I just could not connect the imagined scenarios with the reality. Still, I listened intently. His words seemed to be on a loop, saying the same message only in different ways. Even with Greg's gentle manner and repeated theories, I was having a hard time hearing his words and what the implications were of Sasha's last hours.

"His skeleton is intact, which means he wasn't in a fight. He was just attacked and bled out."

"What do you mean, he was attacked?" I asked numbly but trying to focus. "How could I not know he was so close and suffering?"

"I don't think he suffered. He just needed to go. And I don't think he wanted you to worry."

I had been suffering for a year not knowing about his demise. How could I not know he was thirty feet from my house? How could I not know he was so close and had been decomposing for a year and several months? Why was there just enough orange fur to know it was him? Why was he gone so soon after he had been so sick and had recovered?

Agnieszka reminded me later she heard him that first night we looked for him. Or she thought she had. She thought she heard his voice, his cry, faintly. We were standing on the porch after looking for him that first night he was missing. It was after midnight and Agnieszka was going to leave and drive home, but we decided to call his name again for a few minutes before she left. We were talking quietly and calling his name when Aga thought she heard his voice. We were listening to the quiet Carmel night and hoping to hear something else within the moment but nothing materialized. When she was about to get in her car, she thought about it again and felt she had truly heard something. Yet, she wasn't completely sure, so she decided not to mention it to me a second time. The night had been full of so many false hopes. She didn't want me to be disappointed again. Still, she thought she heard a faint, quiet something, but then there was nothing. Everything is speculative so much later. She blames herself. I blame myself so much more.

In the Box

Sasha was in his box by the shed with a blanket over him. Greg wanted to bury him that same day, but I wasn't ready to deal with his going in the ground just yet. I told Greg I needed some time and he graciously understood. We agreed to bury him at a later date and that I would call him in a few days to set up a burial. Yet, between our schedules it took ten days to find a time that would work for both of us. Sasha was not going anywhere, and neither was I. Debra was in for two weeks, and I didn't want to ruin her visit by having a funeral in the backyard the second day of her visit. We postponed the date, and I felt like I had a reprieve. Deb and I carried on in our yearly ritual. We went to movies and made dinner and ate out. We talked deeply and lightly. She got to know Sophie, as a one-year-old feline now, rebellious, energetic and independent. And all the while Sasha was in a box with a blanket covering him by my shed.

I couldn't look at him. It was too difficult, but it felt good, on some level, to have him next to me and home. Debra and Agnieszka had been extremely supportive, and we knew we had to bury him. Still, I kept putting off the inevitable. I kept walking by the box that held his remains but simply couldn't muster the strength or resolve to peel back the blanket and look at him. I was working a heavy schedule the first half of Deb's visit. She and I were going to Napa Valley in a week, so I was banking hours and trying to get ahead on my work. Management of a high-profile restaurant is a never-ending saga, but I was looking forward to getting away with my sister for a few days and leaving my schedule and well-worn routine behind.

Sasha had been lying in his box next to the shed for almost a week when I finally realized I needed to do what needed to be done. I had to look at him and realize his ending and give myself one as well. I needed to have Greg bury him, and I needed to say goodbye.

I came home from work to my sister and Agnieszka having wine and watching television. They had been out to dinner earlier and were light-hearted in banter and mood. I had some wine with them and then Aga left for home. It was just my sister and I talking. We were thinking about heading for bed and wrapping the day. I had a few glasses of wine by then and decided to do what was needed. Once we pulled out the sleeper sofa and after we had made her bed, I told her I was going to go look at Sasha.

"Don't," she said. "Don't do it. It will just upset you."

"I'm ready," I countered. "I have to do this, and besides, we need to bury him, and I need to say goodbye. I need to see him. He's been out there for days. I'm ready."

She didn't try to stop me. She just looked at me in a sad but supportive way and let out a small sigh. I took a flashlight and turned on the outside light. I was going to take my glasses off, like I used to when I dealt with headless victories and dead squirrels, but decided not to blur the situation any more than I already had. Besides, my night vision is so poor I was probably going to have difficulty seeing him in the Carmel summer fog that had settled over the house throughout the evening.

In the last few days, I had stood over his covered box and tried to will myself to look at him. I came close several times but never pulled back the blanket that separated him from my reality. I walked away and told myself I would look at him tomorrow. There were no other tomorrows. Tonight was for him. Tonight was for him and me completely. But I knew the truth in my heart was more selfish. This moment was what I had been needing and dreading for a long time. The time had come to say goodbye to Sasha. This moment was mostly for me.

I went straight to the box and whispered a prayer for strength. I pulled back the blanket and had trouble focusing my eyes but could just make out a skeleton of outstretched perfection. I was taken aback by how pure and precise the white bones made the form of his body so visibly recognizable. Even though I was looking at physical remains, I had an overwhelming sense of his spirit, of his self. I stood up and walked away. I literally felt a chill go through my body, but I felt strength and wonder also. I looked up into the foggy night, took a deep breath and walked back to the box and knelt down over it.

It was Sasha. There was no doubt. An orange tuft of fur on his forehead gave it all away. His bones were in perfect order. I took an advanced biology class in high school and several of the students chose dissecting a cat as their project. I remember looking at the skinned cats and thinking I could never have a cat if I did that experiment. But then, I never was a cat person before Sal and Sasha. Sasha forever made me feel differently about animals, and on that night I never loved him more. And I loved him always. Despite and because of every single thing we shared and every memory.

I stood over him for a long while. The most disturbing thing was his jaw and how open his mouth was, as though he were screaming. Greg told me the next day, before the burial, that was just the ligaments being gone and the natural position for the bones to progress. My undergraduate degree was in health science, and I took an advanced anatomy class, so I knew that was the correct answer. Still, it was difficult enough to see him in skeleton form because I didn't want to think he was calling for help and I wasn't there for him. The more I knelt over him and took in his remains, the more calming and less disturbing it became, except for the mouth and his beautiful face. Yet, after a while, even his face brought a somewhat peaceful resolve.

I started to speak softly to him because I needed to and because I was still missing him so much. Seeing the ghost of him made me feel him in a different way. It was intimate and surreal and yet more real than I could imagine. And that is what I tried to convey that night in the dark and fog.

"I love you. I love you so much, and I am so sorry. I am so very sorry."

I could feel tears running down my face, and I knew I needed to get inside because Debra was probably worried about me. Yet, once I made peace with seeing him, I didn't want to leave. I knew this would be my last time with him, and I needed to sort out what was in my heart and what I had always felt for him. The last thing I whispered to him that night was my simple truth.

"I miss you so much...still. And I don't think I will ever be the same without you. Thank you for what you brought to my life. I love you so much. Thank you."

I gazed at him one last, long moment then said softly, "Thank you for taking care of me, so very well."

I was crying now, but I felt released and new in a way that was cleansing. I pulled the blanket over his body and went into the cottage. Debra was in bed reading, but I could tell she was waiting for me and monitoring the situation. "Are you okay?" she asked quietly and with a loving look.

"I'm okay," I said as I forced a smile. "It's done. It was good to see him."

I spoke with Debra for a few brief minutes and then went into my room and tried not to cry anymore. And just accept.

I called Greg the next morning and arranged for him to come by as soon as possible to bury him. He came later that day, and we buried Sasha that afternoon.

A Small Grave in the Backyard

Greg came the next day, as promised, by mid-afternoon. Without telling me, he went next door to Glowie and boarded up the missing cinder block area, which had allowed entry under the house, especially for animals. I'm sure Lori told him to do it, but I was touched by his generosity and efficiency in getting it done. I was anxious about having the final closure for Sasha and felt restless all day. Greg might have, as well, because he fixed a light fixture for me and worked on a drain in the house while he waited for Sasha's burial. At four o'clock he took Sasha's remains and dug a more than sufficient hole in the backyard. He placed Sasha delicately and perfectly in the hole. He stood over the burial site for a long time while he waited for us, as if he were protecting sacred ground. I remember thinking it was so noble and valiant of him to be so present. I felt safe in his silent demeanor and quiet control of the burial, and his presence gave me strength.

Earlier in the day, I took some of Sash's favorite toys and strings and put them aside to place in his grave. I had saved all of his toys and bowls and collars in hopes of his return and simultaneously also in memoriam. I told Agnieszka we were going to have the ceremony at four-thirty, but she was running late, and we waited until five for her to arrive. She had flowers and a big spirit, but I was quiet and just wanted to get it done.

Debra was supportive and delicate during the entire afternoon, as she had been throughout her visit. I felt bad that the first part of her visit had been so centered on Sasha's body recovery and now his burial. On some level, we were both just wanting to get it done and frustrated with Agnieszka's late arrival. Yet, Aga made a difference, like she always does. When we got down to it, there were strings and toys laid delicately on his skeleton and soft words spoken. His skeleton had become so real to me now; I could actually see his full form of body, as he had once been in life. In the last twenty-four hours, I had finally become comfortable looking at his bones and could feel him again. His memories and presence felt more vivid and real than ever. It was heartbreaking and life-affirming at the same time.

I said a few words through tears, as did Agnieszka and my sister. I went last and was crying softly and not as articulate as I would have wanted. We said goodbye, and then it was done. Greg covered him, and his strings and toys and bones were one in the dirt, but I didn't stay to watch. I was crying hard by then, yet as silently as I could, but it came in waves and was punishing. I pushed it away as soon as I was able, but I could have let it flow for a long while.

The strings lying next to him were the image that broke my ability to hold back tears. He was only two when he died so young, and his love of strings never ebbed or ceased. He would try to untie my shoestrings even as I was walking in my shoes. He collected any type of string and kept them with his toys. The morning a few years ago when I woke up and discovered he had built a fort out of the throw rugs and had washed his strings and some of my jewelry, laying them out to dry in the middle of the rug structure, was the morning I realized that my life was going to be better eventually. It was the morning I knew I would eventually heal. It was also the moment when I knew how special Sasha was and how deeply I felt for him. When I saw the strings in his grave surrounding him, the sadness and my grief for him overwhelmed. I would never get to hold, care for or love this amazing animal again.

Even though I had Sophie now, at one-year-old and enjoying her young life, Sasha was truly gone forever. There is no comfort from the loss until, finally, there is at least something that resembles less sadness and grief. And that is a lesson I keep learning again and again.

Memories of Funerals Past

I have been to three family funerals in my life. My first was for my brother when I was twenty-five. He was twenty-two when he died in a car crash on a foggy morning in Indiana. A semi-trailer pulled out in front of him on Highway 41 just north of Evansville. Mark was going to work at a construction job, and he died underneath the semi. The driver filed a report with the police and then we never heard from him again. What I remember most about the service at the church was the pew shaking severely. It was shaking because my grandfather was crying so hard. I had never seen him cry before. He was a self-made man and a successful farmer/businessman/Democrat officeholder. He had been close to Mark throughout my brother's childhood. He used to tease my brother to the point of torment, but the torment was always surrounded with love. When I saw my grandfather openly weeping, it made my own sadness seem secondary for a brief moment. Mark's death felt like a waking dream, yet more lucid than anything I had ever experienced at that young age and even to this day. I was his oldest sister. And I always will be.

WHEN HE DIED

morning light filled rented bedroom space
the feeling of euphoria from a strange dream
preoccupies the morning rituals
a flash of white light while getting dressed
danced between myself and my bureau
and took my breath for a brief moment
it is 6:32

smiling slightly at the wonder
something deeper pulls
that I choose to ignore
i move on
out the door, keys in hand
driving to work in early autumn light
because it is what I do
the moving on, the hitting of marks
the obedient actor in my stage play

check in with the photo department
look at footage from a spy plane
i have never seen images from a U-2 plane before
we squint to understand
make comments and jokes
everything is so small
we need a magnifying glass to even recognize
what we can't see or understand

some sort of camaraderie lingers
i am new to them and they to me
a woman in heels directing
what was always military and severe
meet with the film department
the company i work for is making training films
for pilots on how to fly T-37s and T-38s
planes i never knew anything about
until the last three months
when i sat in a simulator in a business suit
and wrecked every plane i attempted to fly

i am twenty-five and living in a strange
but wonderful land called "Texas"
i am learning to drink longnecks, slow down
and learn the warning signs for tornadoes
getting used to sitting in my closet
when the sirens go off and organize my clothes

spending time going to dinners at employees' homes
to make connections
because i was told it would be good
for me to establish relationships with the staff outside of work
because I am so young
and this air force base has never worked with a female
project manager from a contractor before

i sit in their living rooms after dinner
watching slide shows of the wreckage
from five years ago

when the biggest tornado ever recorded
changed their lives forever
realize it is my youth and compassion
that comforts them so
i listen to their stories
but feel their fear
am impressed by their resolve
but can't understand their desire
to hold on to tragedy and fear
for so long

i have a secretary
it is 1984 and she tells me i have a phone call
it is my father
who would never call me at work
or ever really
without something specific to say
or not to say at all

he seems distraught
but there is a strange sense of excitement in his voice
he tells me my brother has been in a bad car accident
he hesitates briefly then tells me
my brother Mark
age 22
is dead
i ask him if he is sure
he says he is absolutely sure
his voice cracks
and it sounds like
a ventriloquist anchoring the news

i cry but don't really shed the tears required
i stare at the pictures in my office
posters and knockoff images
that have nothing to do with him
or my family

i think of my mother
and wonder why my dad called instead of her
i wait for my partner of several years
my first everything
to arrive at work
i try to feel my brother but it is confusing
and yet clear at the same time
after a few moments reality finds me
like blood on bone
alone and wounded
a deep sobbing, thwarted moan
from a place I have never been before

arrangements are made for flying back to Indiana
i have a rare daytime cigarette at the roach coach
and laugh too hard over something ridiculous
unfathomable pain traded for absurdity
love from places not known before
realizing through the fog of shock and incomprehension
the undeniable comprehension of love
from people I have only known for two months
the outpour of their grace sends me home

the plane from dallas having engine trouble
knowing it was not my time

how could that be possible
and feeling cocky in my numbness
at the sheer audacity
in the darkness, looking down
at the small clusters of light in the night
thousands of miles above
my favorite obsession during night flying
the fascination of feeling so many lives
from a safe and uninvolved distance
and the abstract love and confidence
of perspective, solitary and absolute silence

my father picks me up at the small airport in evansville
the struggle for words and conversation
is a physical entity in the car
his overeagerness to bring me to his reality
fuels my exhaustion
he drops my partner and me off at my mom's apartment
after he drives off
i look at the sky and breathe the midwest in autumn
the embrace always soothingly familiar
now unrecognizable

my mother's face, finally
distorted and wrecked
she seems relaxed by something
but i am happy she is numb
she takes my hand and face
and whispers truths and trivial nonsense at the same time
i stay with her until she is taken away
and put in bed

i sleep on a pullout couch
fall asleep to the juxtapositions of images of my flight
the world in lights beyond my control
so beautiful and undefined
and the gaping hole where he used to exist
which is filled now with vulnerability and doubt
profound shock, sadness and grief

in the morning, my mom's best friend is sitting next to me
stroking my head and helping me ease into a morning
of confusion
new territory and strange feelings
choked by the overwhelming
feeling of loss
she holds my hand and gives me everything i need to hear
and tells me through her kindness and words
i can be stronger than i knew possible

my father insists on taking me to the car
to get mark's possessions
he takes my younger brother, age 14, with us
to the wrecking site
where my brother's car is crushed beyond recognition
waiting for us to claim his final moments
and make some sense out of the chaos
all that is evident is
a cooler, some pills, a sandwich
what is felt but not seen is his soul
everything is suddenly
intertwined yet disconnected

blood on the floorboard
blood everywhere
angry at my father for allowing my brother to see this
finding pills and his cooler and a huge bud of sensimilla
my father asking me if it was pot
saying yes and then my father telling me to get rid of it
walking to the fence of the huge wrecking yard
in my texas boots
looking at the weeds and the chain fence
trying to find a place to bury this beautiful bud
then hearing and feeling mark's voice
and knowing he would never, ever want that bud
to be wasted, not to be shared
with those he loved and trusted most
because he shared his entire blueprint life

i stick the plastic bag and long purple-laced beauty
in my new texas boot and walk back to the crushed
bloody metal container my brother died in
"did you get rid of it?" he asked
"yes," I said
my resentment mounting
he looked at me like a cop for a moment
then went back to his searching
for the answers he would never find
his hands so deep in the blood
which was also his

we went through the rest of the car
to find clues or evidence or absolutely anything
which could explain or define

what used to be my brother's life
and despite all of the physical evidence
there was nothing
absolutely nothing to explain the loss
and complete void
of who he used to be and where he was now

there is more
there is always more
everything always moves toward
acquisition or chaos

the "viewing"
a closed casket and a social gathering
my parents holding court
with friends and a small community
the outreach extreme
the context vastly different
my parents embracing
and crying in each other's arms
after a recent divorce
my mother falling apart
knowing it was for real
my father
i never knew for sure
until later

needing so much just to see him
feel his leg or touch some part
of his physical self
which was not distorted or destroyed

watching the tears flow
and feeling angry at all of them
for not understanding
anything but what they brought
which was so minimal
compared to the loss they
didn't even understand
or know

the funeral
my first
my grandfather's tears shaking the pew
a man I never saw cry before
or show any emotion
crying like a child
outside my body
with grief
but completely aware of absolutely everything
feeling worried about everyone
but myself

listening to a stranger speak words
from a pulpit so removed and unsure
yet setting the tone
thinking of my sister's wedding
a month before
and Mark's words to me during the reception
"I had to live my life the way I did"
me dismissing it because he was buzzed
asking him to come back to the party
him wanting time with me

which i gave for a few minutes
then acquiescence to protocol and photo demands
and knowing i should have stayed
with him for so much longer
his look when i got on the plane that weekend
to fly back to texas
a haunting look of love and an eternal goodbye
something in his eyes i had never seen before
that i chose to ignore
but made me stare at him for a long while
as he was smiling from his corner
watching the departure routine
he always smiled
especially when he was young
he would whistle after getting spanked
he smiled constantly
like he was in on a secret
that no one else knew

his last words to me
i can't be sure now
but after watching my sister and me cry through our goodbyes
he looked at me with an ironic smile
and said softly, "i didn't realize you were so close"
"yes, we are now"
i am sure i said, "i love you"
but all that i know with absolute certainty
is the last look i ever saw from him
as i was boarding the plane
he was smiling at me with so much love
like he would never see me again

and it seemed so ridiculous
yet i knew somewhere deep inside of me
he was right

i meant to call him when i got back
to texas and the new world i was so immersed
i thought of him every day
and wanted to talk about the conversation at the reception
but also didn't know how
to venture from that point and give words
to what was so unspoken
yet recognized beyond comprehension
i didn't know how to talk to him
about his pain
but i should have found a way
because i think it could have made a difference somehow
it could have changed all that
was in motion and so beyond control
i was young and eternal and forever
and thought my world was as well
it was not
he was not

not calling him was a bad dream relived for a long while
then gone
like a season changing suddenly
and leaves swept away
nothing that matters is
ever gone or forgotten
one of life's simple truths

learned through tears
so much time has passed now
so many trips around the sun
a thousand moons
but i remember him now most
from my childhood
that is where the conversations reside
and the memories are most vivid
it is where i find him again
smiling and whistling and not yielding
to anything or anyone
but himself

what is a life?
it is everything

it is our living, believable, incredible, unknown,
desirable, perishable
amazing, indescribable
self
and sometimes
it ends before it has barely begun.

A VINTAGE FLYING SAUCER

Funerals Past

THE THIRD FUNERAL I ATTENDED WAS FOR ERIC PAUL, who died at thirty-nine, though we could never confirm his age definitely (and he would never want us to get that number). What I remember most about his service at the Mission Ranch was Alix getting up to give the first speech about her first memory of him. Her story about a vintage flying saucer borrowed from an art house in San Francisco, lost after flying off of his rented truck over Hollister, intended for a Christmas display that he was creating at Sierra Mar, and my calling her to talk him down while he was frantically running along a busy highway, and that I asked her to intervene when she didn't even know him, brought the house down. After her story, everyone lined up to tell a memory, a story, an afterthought. Yet, she made that happen with the first rousing, touching ancedote.

Her inspiring words initiated a burst of enthusiastic and inspired people coming forward to share their memories of him. I loved her so deeply for the courage to get such a party started by standing up first and talking from her heart. To this day, I love her so much for that single moment. So many people came forward to tell stories that there was a line waiting to get to the podium. I felt too wrecked to share my words, and as I sat there listening to so many great stories and moments from people, I slowly realized I was not able or willing to give them any of my feelings or moments about him. They were mine, and I was too sorrowful and angry to share them with those who were there and loved him so much because they wanted more. And I did as well.

ASHES AND RAIN

I'VE BEEN THINKING ABOUT YOU FOR WEEKS NOW. You seem a bit playful to me, but I know you have my best interests at heart. It is Easter Sunday and it is colder than I can ever remember for April. I was driving to work today thinking of you and remembering your pretense of loathing this holiday and then also remembering how you indulged others with the candy and the flowers and the little eggs you seemed to hate. I always admired your deft hand in the situations that made you uncomfortable.

It started storming early in the afternoon and has not let up. It is late in the evening now, and the rain is still pouring down on my cottage. I am determined to take some of you to the beach. This is your day, after all, and the rain has ceased for a moment. I draw myself in and put myself in raingear and gather a small part of you for the journey to the beach. I keep you under the alcove in my desk normally. I have not looked at your ashes in a year. I take you out of the box, which holds Jose's special tin, and pour a fragment of you into a Ziplock baggie. This is my big moment, careful to not spread you on the carpet and trying not to be worried about the sanitary ramifications. Have I become you?

I start walking to the beach, and the rain commences like a long-lost relative eager to make up for lost time. I keep walking but am becoming thoroughly drenched. I make a new plan and walk the two blocks back to the car. I had a glass of wine after work, and all of my decisions in the downpour seem to be based on staying safe yet reckless. I am caught in the tumbler of my contradictions. Still, I take you to the car and drive to the beach such a short distance from my house. When I get there, the wind is pummeling, and the rain is coming down in sheets. I walk to the edge of the beach but realize the wind will only throw you back in my face. Even though I can't see the surf because of the rain and fog, the ocean is roaring and makes for the dramatic flare I know you would love. I take you back to the car and ask simply, "Where do you want to be?"

Your answer seems swift and clear. Hurricane Point or Sierra Mar Restaurant. I leave you in the car and get completely soaked getting back to the house. You are in a Ziplock, hopefully not fully knowing you have been left in the car overnight. But at least now you know I have a Lexus. Toward the end, you were worried about my next car purchase. You were very clear about not getting a 7 series BMW, even though I could not have afforded the one I wanted. You told me I was too young to be that old. The Lexus was a great deal, and even though I bought it used online, it has been fairly respectable toward me. After witnessing your horror stories of buying two cars online, and having lived through the consequences of carpooling in those two vehicles, I was incredibly skeptical about the whole affair. I once said that your affection toward your cars was based on how much abuse they would take under your tutelage. I don't think I ever carpooled with you in a vehicle that didn't smell of oil, gas or distrust.

Tomorrow I will take you to Big Sur. One last carpool, in a way. I will probably feel too much. I always do once I allow myself to remember, but it is bittersweet in some ways now. On a good day it can feel like the ticklish sensation you get in your stomach after you have been spinning very fast in circles and you are just starting to feel dizzy. You can't help but smile in that moment because nothing else matters for a second except for the feeling of falling, free and clear and out of control from the world. For one brief moment, you have no control and it feels so good, just for a second or two, to succumb to the chaos.

I think you were the first person I knew who used chaos as an effective tool to keep people guessing and off balance. Chaos was your fictional reality. It was your refuge, comic relief and sleight of hand. The truth is you kept your house in immaculate order; chaos was just your border patrol. Tangibles were never left to chance until the end, where they will remain so for infinity. You could counsel, critique and observe better than anyone I have ever known. You withheld and hinted and peppered the truth more than I could sometimes tolerate. You created mysticism and mystery in your chaos, but it was your structured order that held your soul.

By now, I hope you know I ended up taking you to Big Sur the next day. I let your ashes go high over the Pacific at the restaurant you loved so much. I was careful to understand the direction of the wind, but I still ended up with some of you in my hair and face because of a sudden gust from a different direction. I realized at that moment you still always get your way, and it made me smile. I wish I could tell you Jose is okay, but he is not really. He moves forward in his time and place. He bought a different house. He is still taking care of his mother, whom he loves so much, but there is a loneliness in his voice that sounds like an echo, and it reverberates and dies a quiet death in all of our interactions. It is the sound of his love for you, and when I hear it, I know that I am no longer too young to be old.

QUESTIONS WITHOUT ANSWERS...ANSWERS WITH QUESTIONS

Life Without and Within

When loss happens, it is all that exists. Sasha was gone. I had closure without knowing. I had a funeral. I knew an ending in a vague way. But I didn't have answers. And answers are crucial for me. They are a language I understand and respect. I didn't know how Sasha died or what caused his death. As much as I finally accepted the outcome, I didn't have a conclusion or comprehension as to his demise and loss. In a strange way, that singular unknown was one of the most difficult things to understand in two years of so much loss and pain. I realized after measured time, sometimes there simply are no answers. And that was my eventual gift and my eternal struggle.

I don't understand the mysteries of the universe, yet I believe they exist. I am just not privy to the language. Still, I believe mystery and fate have consequence more than we acknowledge or believe. There are too many random acts of fate and outcomes that are difficult to explain or find meaning in, and, yet, they are revealed years later. I believe in coincidences and random connections with meanings. I believe in love and a higher-power playing field. I wanted to know why Sasha died and how he met that outcome. I wanted to understand because I have never understood why so much loss can come so quickly and without reason.

The Long Game and Life with Angels

Sasha was buried in the backyard beneath a hydrangea bush that is finally blooming. Life went grandly yet gently forward, even though everything was different, and yet in some ways it wasn't. I still feel him. I still feel all of them. My guardians now, I suppose. I know they always have my best interest at heart. There have been too many instances in which I was saved from harm's way for me not to believe in their power to shed light and protection on my life.

The car accident years ago with Alix, when we were both starting new jobs in 1996, comes prominently to mind. She was on her first road trip with her new position as a wine rep. I urged her to take me with her to Paso Robles because I had a feeling. She agreed, reluctantly, the morning she was to leave. All day I was feeling disconnected from my physical body. I went to a used bookstore while she was cold-calling on restaurants, and when she picked me up, I was light and immersed in my book purchases. When the accident happened, when a young kid ran a stoplight, I was looking at my books and strangely euphoric. I heard her scream in a calm, controlled but scared way. All I felt at the moment of impact was the sensation of white light surrounding me. The moment felt like we had gone through an amusement ride in slow motion. Alix suffered a concussion. I felt nothing and had no injuries. It was strange because the visor I was wearing was crushed. (Yes, I actually had a brief period when I wore a visor to pull back my hair.) After the white light, I had no taste for meat and became a vegetarian for a few years. I'm not sure of the ramifications, but the outcome was specific.

The white light in my dashboard driving to San Francisco with Agnieszka in that fateful worst year of my life, when I didn't know her at all and was giving her a ride to the city, created a calm for me when a mattress flew into my dashboard at 80 mph in six lanes of rush hour traffic. We could have been killed, but we weren't. A small voice in my head told me emphatically to stay in my lane. The mattress blocked the entire front window. I was able to pull over by using the side mirror of my vintage BMW station wagon. Agnieszka's head could have been severed from the impact and the placement of the mattress frame beam, but she wasn't harmed in any way. The beam missed her by two inches. It was how our friendship began. After I was able to finally pull the car over to the shoulder of the road in six lanes of fast-moving vehicles, and we were shaking from the shock of the situation, she looked at me intensely and said with Polish firmness, "Your life is trying to tell you something." And then, after laughing for a brief moment because of the absurdity of the situation, I cried tears of relief and disbelief. The CHP who eventually showed up and helped us told me he didn't know how I avoided a massive pile-up. Survival is extremely powerful. And the accident was a pivotal turning point.

My radio turning itself on one Valentine's Day driving to work in Big Sur during the terrible year of 2005, when I didn't think I could be alone with all of it anymore. And the song it was playing took my breath away because it was impossible that it had happened. And it had to be him.

Talking on the phone one night and hearing loud, heavy foot-steps running through the living room in such a playful way and suddenly being overcome with the feeling of Sasha being present. The loud footsteps were real, but nothing else about the experience was grounded in reality, except that it absolutely happened. And Sophie validated the moment with her look of shock, confusion and concern.

Getting my house in Carmel when there was no reason for me even to know about the listing, until Alix did and went and looked at the cottage and told me it was perfect for me. Even though there were sixty people before me on the register, the owners still picked me so late in the process.

Finding Sasha, though I had no inclination of ever being a guardian for a cat in my lifetime, and the insistence of the Hurricane on my giving him a home. Finding Sophie when I wasn't looking for another cat because I was afraid of more heartache.

Seeing so many meteors driving home from Big Sur and so many meteors from the cottage when I needed to see them most. The white owl at Molera, which occasionally seemed to want to take my head off, even though I am driving a vehicle that could kill it. And seeing that white owl again and again, especially when I wasn't expecting it, but its presence making a difference, somehow, and making me wonder about the wonder in everything. Moments I can't explain through natural discourse or logic. And I don't try anymore. I just accept. And that has made all the difference. In this gifted, grateful life.

ALWAYS...FOREVER

WHAT IS LOVE? It is the eternal question and the infinite answer. It comes in the tickle of an arm slightly touched. It comes in whispers and nuances. It is the sound of the surf breaking outside my house in Carmel. It is the light of autumn when the mood of life begins to change, and everything turns toward the deep memories of love. It is the early morning light in a quaint cottage built in 1945 that is mine to savor. It is the look across a room of friends and strangers from the one who makes all the difference, which means you are more important than any single thing or moment. It is given when it is not expected or sometimes not ready to be received. It is juice brought to you on a tray with a bendy straw when you are in bed sick with the flu. It is laughter and promise and desire and the culmination of a perfect day. It comes in an orange cat that lies on your arms as you read while he sleeps without guilt or purpose or plan. It is the way my staff looks at me when I come into work. It is the way they look at me always. It is the whisper that surrounds us, and the comfort we can't define. It is the humor and muse and hope when there is no other reason to pursue.

What is love? Her breath on my neck. Her voice in my ear, speaking softly, knowing it is true. Dinner and conversations that span a lifetime in real time. Orion above you while you listen to the night. The stillness when you are alone with yourself and need answers. Being alone, especially late at night, when everything bears down, and there is only you to manage the debris and the expectation and still feel what is needed. It is finding solace in what matters and knowing the difference in what is not worth the worry. It is the sound of your own breath when you think you can't breathe.

What is love? Breakfast in the window nook listening for Sophie. Sasha always. My immortal family. Aga being true to herself and living fearlessly and without boundaries. The Hurricane in a red bedroom. Eric Paul's long-lashed eyes and the way they looked at me. His last breath and the look in his eyes when he left his life. My grandmother's voice humming while she ironed clothes listening to old jazz on the radio. Alix and thousands of moments. Her deft intimacy and humor. The knowing and the unknown and the search to understand. Mark and his joy as a child, and whistling, even when the moment was not worth a song. My father lifting me up and making me dream of flying.

In this life. In this moment. Everything. And more.

And for some inexplicable, unexplainable, incomprehensible reason, an orange tabby cat with a unique voice and indomitable spirit made me understand what was needed and what I was destined to finally understand.

What is love? It is the mystery of the universe. And the mystery of us.

ACKNOWLEDGEMENTS

I ENJOY READING THE ACKNOWLEDGEMENT SECTION of books, especially books that draw me in completely and provide an intimate reading experience. When I read those pages, I am grateful to know more about how the book came to be and who played a role in making the book happen. I also think how difficult it must be to write that section of a book. How do you ever find a way to thank everyone who helped guide the writing process and journey? Now I am feeling that burden and joy. Truth is, I never thought I would be in this position. Writing was always a passion but something that was mostly mine alone. Publishing was always a goal but more of a dream. I certainly never thought I would publish a book about a cat, but sometimes life intervenes.

The first people outside my inner circle to take my book seriously and push me to publish were Linda Lannon and Michael Thiery during a conversation on the deck of Sierra Mar during my last year as general manager of the restaurant. Having worked in publishing, their interest, guidance and enthusiasm gave me small doses of much-needed confidence when I was working on my first rewrite and just beginning to understand where the book was taking me. Linda, thank you for the many SNST meetings over the past few years shared over a glass of wine.

I would like to thank some of my first readers, who include Myrna Reynolds, Lauren DaCruz, Lori Trew, Gloria Dougherty, Alyssa Dougherty, Amanda Feldman, Lucinda McDermott, Melissa Snyder, Tammy Chesney, Bettina Gordon and Sarah Kabat-Marcy. Even though the bones of the book were evident, the writing was in the earliest stages. Yet, their enthusiastic encouragement eased my anxiety about revealing such personal work. With each new read of the book, by each new person, I slowly developed more confidence and a growing, quiet determination. I am so grateful for their tender love and support.

I would also like to thank some of my later readers as the book went through smaller changes toward finishing, who include JoAnne Hellwig, Patricia Galli, Jane Ponchione, Jackie Pelosi, Robin Fagundes, Kate Rider, Pedro Mendosa, Sheri Lebositz and Stacey Clapp. My later readers made me realize I won't necessarily die if I take my clothes off in public. Thank you for your intensely personal and emotional comments and shares. You made the book and me better because of the depth of your honesty.

I would like to express extreme gratitude to Lauren Alwan who took me on as a client and edited the first two drafts of the book. Her insight, patience and belief in the early work made all the difference and I learned volumes from her every time we met. I want to give deep heartfelt thanks to my cousin Peg Alford Pursell for her guidance, candor and unique perspective on everything that matters. I am in awe of your talent, and your books inspired me to be more fearless about my own writing and life. I am incredibly grateful to have found Chris Molé, graphic designer, through happenstance, which proved to be predetermined and fateful. I'm not sure I could have finished the book without your guidance, grace and patience. I am indebted to Cheryl Winningham for sculpting the book cover design and bringing her skill and professional standard to my small, but meaningful, project.

I want thank my good friend Tricia Perault for decades of friendship and for changing the course of my life when she and her husband, Tony, hired me at Sierra Mar in 1996. How fortunate am I that she also possesses a razor-edge editing and proofreading ability and was the last person to make the necessary changes to the book. She made the book immensely better and my writing as well.

I want to thank Karuna Licht for giving me the skills to find my voice…and my life. You left too soon, and I miss you terribly.

Jose Ruvalcaba thank you for being the courageous, kind-hearted loving person you have always been and for loving Eric so well, taking such good care of him and making him so happy.

I am grateful to my family for their love and support through years of on-and-off again writing, revisions and changes. Mom, Debra and "Seth," you've made all the difference my entire life. Thank you.

I am thankful for my other family, the meaningful mercurial satellites in my orbit who make the journey more interesting, entertaining and joyful, always, especially this past difficult year. Thank you, Agnieszka Kaźmierczak, Beatriz Avila, Amanda Feldman, Kate and Kevin Rider, Gloria and Jim Dougherty, Alyssa Dougherty, Toni Nicklaus, Tony and Tricia Perault, Bettina Gordon, Brooke Ramondo, Sarah Kabat-Marcy, Tim and Carla Riordan, Lori Trew, Todd Williamson and my Rancho Cielo family: Mark, Susie, EJ, Laura, Carla and Kristina.

And lastly, thank you to Agnieszka Kaźmierczak for believing steadfastly and unwaveringly in this book from the moment you read an early chapter through every draft, momentum shift and milestone met. You never let me give up on bringing the book to fruition, and you never gave up on me. I simply can't imagine this journey without your emotional support, deep friendship and love. I am so incredibly grateful for your artistic design, photography and artwork in making the book cover match my vision. Thank you for keeping me in farm-fresh eggs and other sundries when things were lean, and I was focusing on finishing the story. Thank you for being present for all of it, every moment. You are truly one of my angels.

WANDA STRAW grew up in Western Pennsylvania and moved to Southern Indiana when she was sixteen. After receiving an MA in telecommunications, she managed numerous projects in several different states for a media defense contractor. She moved to the Monterey Peninsula in California in 1987, managing a contract at the Defense Language Institute. She spent 19 years at Sierra Mar Restaurant at the Post Ranch Inn in Big Sur, with nearly 16 years as the general manager. Wanda is currently working on a book of short stories about the food and wine industry entitled *Julia Child Said My Name*. Carmel has been her home for fifteen years. *Sasha Noodle String Theory* is her first book.

Made in the USA
Las Vegas, NV
13 November 2022

59354272R00144